INTENSIFYING CARE:
The Hospital Industry,
Professionalization,
and the Reorganization of
the Nursing Labor Process

Robert L. Brannon

Critical Approaches in the Health Social Sciences Series
Series Editor: Ray H. Elling

Baywood Publishing Company, Inc.
AMITYVILLE, NEW YORK

Library of Congress Catalog Number: 94-11059
ISBN: 0-89503-162-0 (paper)
ISBN: 0-89503-161-2 (cloth)

Library of Congress Cataloging-in-Publication Data

Brannon, Robert L.
  Intensifying care : the hospital industry, professionalization, and the reorganization of the nursing labor process / Robert L. Brannon.
      p.   cm. - - (Critical approaches in the health social sciences series)
  Includes bibliographical references and index.
  ISBN 0-89503-161-2. - - ISBN 0-89503-162-0 (pbk.)
  1. Nursing- -Practice- -Social aspects- -United States.
2. Industrial sociology- -Case studies. 3. Nurses- -United States-
-Job descriptions. 4. Primary nursing- -United States. 5. Team
nursing- -United States. I. Title. II. Series.
  [DNLM: 1. Primary Nursing Care- -organization & administration.
2. Medical Staff, Hospital- -organization & administration.
3. Nursing- -trends- -United States. WY 101 B821i 1994]
RT86.73.B73 1994
610.73'0973- -dc20
DNLM/DLC
for Library of Congress   94-11059
                                                              CIP

Acknowledgments

This book began as a doctoral dissertation in sociology at the University of California, Berkeley. I would like to thank Michael Reich, Franz Schurmann, and Neil Smelser for their comments, criticism, and encouragement to pursue publication of the study as a book. I would also like to thank Don Holloway, whose project in the School of Public Health introduced me to health care research.

The book itself is an entirely rewritten document that includes new research. I am indebted to the scholars whose work directly influenced my own, which encompasses both medical sociology and the sociology of work, occupations and professions. They are indicated in numerous citations. I have benefitted by presenting parts of my research at professional meetings and appreciate the comments of organizers and discussants, including Jacqueline Boles, Chris Hope, Sylvia Kenig, Ronald Pavalko, and Edward Ransford. Faculty research fellowships at the University of Kentucky supported additional research and the rewriting of the manuscript. My move to Kentucky also provided the opportunity to become acquainted with two prominent medical sociologists whose work I admire—Eugene Gallagher and Robert Straus.

I want to thank Sylvia Kenig, Ray H. Elling, Series Editor, and Stuart Cohen and the staff of Baywood Publishing Company for their help and advice in getting the manuscript into print. I also thank anonymous reviewers for their time and comments.

My greatest appreciation goes to my wife Dorothy Peters-Brannon, R.N., who not only lived the case study experience at "Pacific Hospital" with me, but contributed significantly by reading and commenting on numerous drafts of the manuscript. Our daughter Louisa, born during the early stages of the research, has been more understanding than we had the right to expect and contributed in her own charming way.

Finally, I would like to thank my former coworkers, the nurses and hospital workers with whom I shared many hours on the wards.

Contents

Introduction

Health care is one of the largest industries in the United States. Between 1945 and 1990, national health care expenditures grew from 4 to over 12 percent of gross national product, and the number of workers employed in the industry reached over nine million [1]. While this period of expansion stretches over four decades, for health care providers, the 1950s and 1960s may have been the industry's golden age. During these decades the postwar economy was booming, and community hospitals added new technology, larger facilities, and a burgeoning work force of professional and technical workers to assist physicians in the care of their patients. The health care industry seemed to exemplify a developing postindustrial society under the control of professionals. As the dominant profession in health care, physicians not only commanded a hierarchy of subordinate occupations but shared in the governance of hospitals. Relations between administrators and physicians could be characterized as "dynamics without change" [2].

Health care continued to expand in the 1970s and 1980s, but the centrality of community hospitals and the power of the medical profession were contested by the efforts of non-health care corporations and the state to contain rising health care costs. As the major purchasers of services challenged the providers, the industry entered a period of significant social change. The term "corporatization" has been used to characterize the entrance of large capitalist corporations into the production of medical services, the development of alternative provider organizations, and the reorganization of community hospitals through the introduction of more rationalized systems of management and bureaucratic control. Because corporatization markedly strengthens the power of administrators, the restructuring of the industry has been discussed largely in terms of its effect on physicians' power and occupational status, producing an extensive debate as to whether physicians are experiencing professional decline [3].

While studies of corporatization have focused on the reorganization of institutions and the restructuring of power among elite groups, the effect on subordinate health care occupations—nurses, paraprofessionals, and nonprofessional workers—has received far less attention. As Renee Fox has noted, when questions about these workers have been addressed, sociologists often rely on research completed in prior decades and, in the case of nursing, on studies conducted by the nursing profession itself. When we consider that the majority of patient care is produced by semiprofessional and paraprofessional workers, it is surprising that medical sociologists have neglected these workers in recent studies of changes in the industry [4].

Among the diversity of occupations engaged in the production of health care services, nurses are the largest occupational group [5]. Not only is nursing care one of the principal services that hospitals produce, the ongoing sociological debate surrounding the effects of corporatization on the medical profession may be more applicable to nursing than to medicine. Throughout this century, the professional status of nurses has been less secure than that of physicians. Considered a semiprofession by occupational sociologists, nursing would seem more susceptible to either upgrading or downgrading as the industry changes [6].

This study helps remedy the lack of attention given subordinate health care occupations by examining the reorganization of nursing during the contemporary period of corporatization and cost containment. It links changes in the occupation and the organization of work on hospital wards with larger changes in the industry. Whereas the reorganization of nursing cannot be adequately understood without attention to the political economy of health care, the corporatization of community hospitals, and new strategies for managing subordinate workers, our understanding of recent changes in the health care industry is seriously amiss if we overlook the reorganization of the division of labor on hospital wards—the central work process in hospitals and in the industry, for that matter.

In focusing on the reorganization of nursing work, I pursue a sociological analysis of the transition from "team nursing," in the expansionary decades of the 1950s and 1960s to variations of "primary nursing" and a trend toward an all-RN nursing staff in the 1970s and 1980s, a transition that occurred along with the changes in the political economy of the industry. In response to greater market competition and pressures to contain costs, community hospitals not only transformed themselves into diversified health care corporations, corporate managers reorganized the work of hospital workers to contain labor costs and increase productivity [7]. Nursing was at the center of these changes.

The reorganization of nursing is of particular interest sociologically because team and primary nursing exemplify fundamentally different and even opposing means of organizing the division of labor. Team nursing was based on a differentiation of tasks among a stratified work force of registered nurses (RNs), licensed practical nurses (LPNs), and nurses' aides [8]. "Auxiliaries," as LPNs and aides were labeled by nursing administrators in the 1950s and 1960s, worked in teams supervised by RNs, who were responsible for overall nursing care and for the more technical tasks that seemed appropriately assigned to the professional nurse. LPNs and aides were delegated the routine tasks that required a greater presence at the bedside. During the 1970s and 1980s, the team approach was replaced by primary nursing and a trend toward an all-RN work force. In contrast to team nursing, tasks were now reunified. RNs performed what nursing leaders called "total patient care" and had an unmediated relationship with their patients. As hospitals implemented "primary nursing" (which I use as a generic term that includes considerable variation in practice), LPNs and nurses' aides were largely displaced to other departments in hospitals and to work sites on the periphery of hospitals, in nursing homes, rehabilitation hospitals, home health care, and clinics [9].

While examining this major change at the center of the health care industry, the study addresses issues of theoretical importance to the sociology of occupations and professions generally. First, my focus is on changes in the division of labor, a subject of long-standing interest to sociologists. However, unlike many other studies of occupations, my attention is on the organization of work. Research on health care occupations has contributed more to our knowledge of the *occupational* division of labor than to the actual organization of work in particular production processes in health care institutions, that is, the labor process. Few studies examine how or why the division of labor in these settings change [10].

A second theoretical issues involves the various interests that must be taken into account in understanding changes in the organization of professional work. Sociologists of work often study jobs that are tailored to managerial interests in achieving economic efficiency and the control necessary to direct workers toward administratively established goals. In these "occupations," workers' capacity to control their work is limited, whereas in professional work, occupational interests are expected to play a more significant role as professionals presumably have greater control over their work [11].

Nursing, however, is usually viewed as a semiprofession firmly subordinated to physicians' professional dominance and to administrators' bureaucratic control [12]. One could easily assume that the organization of nurses' work is determined by these elites. I will show that even with the recent corporatization of hospitals, the reorganization of nursing cannot be explained simply through the interests of administrators or physicians. Although nurses do not escape elite domination, nursing's occupational interests must be considered as well. I will argue that changes in the organization of nursing labor have resulted from a convergence of occupational and managerial interests at particular phases in the historical development of the occupation and the industry.

Furthermore, it is important to distinguish between the professionalization project of nursing leaders and the experience of rank and file nurses on hospital wards. The motivations and consciousness of the latter do not necessarily match those of nursing educators and administrators. Thus, in examining the reorganization of nursing, I not only consider managerial and elite occupational interests but how the organization of work on hospital wards generates cooperation with or resistance to changes initiated from above.

I am particularly concerned with a third and related issue, namely how we interpret the reorganization of nursing labor. To put the matter directly, did the transition from team to primary nursing professionalize or deprofessionalize and perhaps even proletarianize nursing? With corporatization and a growing health care cost crisis, one might expect deprofessionalization or proletarianization, since the majority of nurses work in hospitals and are subject to bureaucratic control and the policies of administrators. Nonetheless, as with claims to the attainment of professional status, we should not assume that this is the case. Indeed, the prevailing view among nursing leaders was that primary nursing and the trend toward an all-RN labor force professionalized the occupation.

In promoting primary nursing in the 1970s and 1980s, nursing leaders maintained that hospital employment and team nursing with auxiliaries deprofessionalized nursing by subdividing tasks and fragmenting care, destroying the integrity of RNs' professional practice [13]. This interpretation can be supported by the sociological literature on professional decline which argues that employment in bureaucratic settings often results in the attenuation of professional autonomy and control. Managers are said to dominate professional workers, who are then deprofessionalized or proletarianized. Work may be subdivided and cheaper workers hired to perform less skilled tasks. Semiprofessional occupations, particularly, may be subject to proletarianization as capitalist social relations permeate industries like health care [14].

Nursing leaders argued that primary nursing would reprofessionalize nursing work by reunifying tasks and creating an unmediated relationship between the RN and the patient. They claimed that primary nursing was based on professional principles that had existed in "private duty" nursing before RNs or auxiliaries were ever employed by hospitals [15]. Prior to the postwar period, hospital nursing was produced by apprentices who staffed the wards while completing their training in hospital-based schools. The majority of "graduate nurses" (later called RNs, with registration and licensing) worked in private duty, where the nurse had a one-to-one relationship with a patient and performed their complete nursing care. Advocates of primary nursing claimed that with RNs' employment in hospitals beginning in the 1930s, professional nurses eventually replaced apprentices only to be deprofessionalized by the subdivision of nursing work and the widespread hiring of auxiliaries [16].

This interpretation raises interesting empirical and theoretical questions. The deprofessionalization or proletarianization of nursing is said to have occurred during the expansionary decades of the 1950s and 1960s, while the reprofessionalization of the occupation is supposed to have occurred during the cost containment period. As mentioned earlier, with the corporatization of hospitals and the cost crisis, one might reasonably expect just the opposite.

Moreover, this interpretation contradicts major sociological theories of professionalization and proletarianization. Contrary to the claim that reunifying tasks professionalizes nursing, sociological theories maintain that as occupations professionalize, they typically differentiate upgraded tasks from routine tasks that can be delegated to paraprofessional or nonprofessional workers [17]. From this perspective, nursing's recent pursuit of professionalization through reunified tasks would appear to be an anomaly. In fact, sociological studies of the division of labor on hospital wards during the 1950s, including important studies by Everett Hughes and his associates, argued that the differentiation of tasks in *team nursing* demonstrated the process of professionalization [18]. If team nursing upgraded nurses' tasks, a dedifferentiation of tasks would reverse the professionalization process and contradict occupational interests. Why would nursing leaders want RNs to take back routine tasks? And why would RNs cooperate?

Reunifying tasks also contradicts sociological theories of proletarianization that are based on management's subdivision of work and the assignment of degraded tasks to less skilled, cheaper workers. In reunifying tasks, primary nursing reverses an organization of work that has often been associated with efficiency, economy, and managerial control [19]. Administrators can no longer assign the bulk of routine tasks to less expensive workers. If team nursing served managerial interests, why would managers reunify tasks, employ more RNs, and displace auxiliaries?

To understand the reorganization of the division of labor and to answer questions raised by competing theories and interests, I began what eventually became the major part of the study, a comparative analysis of nursing labor in which I examine the major features of each type of work pattern. To understand the organization of team nursing in the immediate postwar period, I examined what appeared by the amount of dust on the volumes to be a largely forgotten sociological literature on nursing, completed in the 1950s. And, because nursing leaders claimed that team nursing had deprofessionalized the occupation and that primary nursing would reprofessionalize it by returning to earlier principles of organizing work, it was necessary to analyze prior forms of labor. Recent social histories of nursing as well as reports on the status of nursing in the 1920s provided material for assessing hospital apprenticeship and private duty, the antecedents to RNs' employment in hospitals.

However, my interest in the reorganization of nursing labor did not originate in libraries but from observations on hospital wards. Between 1979 and 1988 I worked part-time for several periods at a California hospital in the San Francisco Bay area that I will refer to by the pseudonym of "Pacific Hospital," to maintain the institution's anonymity. While working as a ward clerk, the only non-nursing worker continuously on the wards, I observed first hand both the corporatization of the hospital and the reorganization of work. During my employment, hospital elites transformed a community hospital into a diversified health care corporation, creating new businesses on the periphery of the hospital. The rise of corporate managers altered the balance of power with physicians and the board of trustees, and new managerial strategies were soon implemented to contain labor costs and increase productivity among subordinate workers. From my position on the wards, I was able to document the effect on nurses and the hospital's central work process.

Pacific Hospital was known in the industry for its advanced nursing practice. The hospital had begun shifting to primary nursing and an all-RN work force in the early 1970s. Staffing with LPNs and nurses' aides declined, so that by the mid-1980s RNs clearly predominated, a dramatic reversal from prior decades in which the majority of the nursing staff were LPNs and aides working under the supervision of RNs.

As I pursued research on prior forms of nursing labor I worked on the wards observing the reorganization of work and its effects on nurses. My observations led me to address related issues as well, including how social relations between RNs and ancillary workers providing various support services were affected by the change.

I also became interested in the effects of reorganizing nursing labor on workers' empowerment. The majority of hospital workers were women, which provided a basis for workplace solidarity. However, workers were divided by occupation, social class, and race. Following patterns in the industry, RNs and paraprofessional workers were likely to have mixed class backgrounds (middle and working class) and were overwhelmingly white. The majority of nonprofessional workers were also white, but they were more likely to come from the working class, and racial minorities were overrepresented in these occupations [20]. Furthermore, although RNs, auxiliary nurses, and most support workers were organized for collective bargaining, they were divided by differing strategies of empowerment. RNs were represented by the California Nurses' Association (CNA), a progressive branch of the American Nurses' Association (ANA) that combined collective bargaining with a commitment to advancing the professional interests of RNs. LPNs and nurses' aides, along with other nonprofessional workers (including ward clerks), were represented by the Service Employees International Union (SEIU), which organized workers across job categories. While most workers did not participate in the activities of either organization except during periods in which contracts were being renegotiated, activists in SEIU suggested to me that management may have displaced auxiliary nurses to weaken the union.

Part One of this study discusses social changes in the industry and the transformation of community hospitals. In Chapter 1, I treat the historical development of the industry and the changing political economy that led non-health care corporations and the state to pressure hospitals to contain costs. Chapter 2 discusses the response of community hospitals to these pressures: the corporatization of hospitals, the restructuring of the governing elite, and the reorganization of work among hospital workers. I use material from my case study of Pacific Hospital to illustrate these changes.

Part Two consists of a comparative study of the different forms of nursing labor relevant to understanding the reorganization of work on hospital wards during the contemporary cost containment era. In Chapter 3, I examine hospital apprenticeship and private duty, which provides a basis for assessing claims that team nursing deprofessionalized nursing practice, and that primary nursing reprofessionalizes the occupation by returning to principles of work that existed in private duty. In Chapter 4, team nursing and the differentiation of nursing tasks in the immediate postwar decades are discussed. In reinterpreting team nursing, I critique sociological studies of professionalization completed in the 1950s as well as recent claims of nursing's deprofessionalization through subdivided work. Chapter 5 examines the development of primary nursing during the cost containment era that began in the 1970s and 1980s. After considering the argument that primary nursing reprofessionalizes the occupation, in an extended case study of the reorganization of work at Pacific Hospital I reveal both its attraction for ward nurses and the subsequent costs involved. In the Conclusion and Epilogue, I summarize the argument, discuss the theoretical implications, and consider more recent trends in the organization of nursing labor as the health care industry moves toward a new century.

NOTES

1. National Center for Health Statistics, *Health, United States, 1991* (Hyattsville, Md.: Public Health Service, 1992), tables 95, 112.
2. Robert R. Alford, "The Political Economy of Health Care: Dynamics without Change," *Politics and Society* 2 (Winter 1972): 127-164.
3. Paul Starr, *The Social Transformation of American Medicine* (New York: Basic Books, 1982); Linda A. Bergthold, *Purchasing Power in Health* (New Brunswick: Rutgers University Press, 1990); The Changing Character of the Medical Profession [special issue] *Milbank Quarterly* 66(supplement 2) (1988). Also, my discussion in chap. 2.

4. Renee C. Fox, "Reflections and Opportunities in the Sociology of Medicine," *Journal of Health and Social Behavior* 26 (March 1985): 6-14.
5. Nancy Aries and Louanne Kennedy, "The Health Labor Force: The Effects of Change," in *The Sociology of Health and Illness,* ed. Peter Conrad and Rochelle Kern, 3rd ed. (New York: St. Martin's Press, 1990), 200.
6. Amitai Etzioni, ed., *The Semi-Professions and Their Organization* (New York: Free Press, 1969); George Ritzer and David Walczak, *Working: Conflict and Change,* 3rd ed. (Englewood Cliffs, N.J.: Prentice-Hall, 1986), chap. 9.
7. I discuss these changes in detail in chap. 2.
8. In some states, licensed practical nurses (LPNs) are referred to as licensed vocational nurses or LVNs. I have adhered to the term LPN because it is more commonly used throughout the country.
9. The reorganization of work included not simply shifting paid workers from hospitals to wage labor in diversified work settings such as nursing homes and clinics, but to unpaid labor in the home. See Nona Y. Glazer, "Overlooked, Overworked: Women's Unpaid and Paid Work in the Health Services' 'Cost Crisis'," *International Journal of Health Services* 18(1) (1988): 119-137.
10. See Glenn Gritzer and Arnold Arluke, *The Making of Rehabilitation* (Berkeley: University of California Press, 1985), xii. The Foreword by Eliot Freidson provides a useful discussion of the occupational division of labor in health care as does the case study that follows. Additional recent studies include Sydney A. Halpern's *American Pediatrics* (Berkeley: University of California Press, 1988), which contributes to our understanding of a particular type of occupational differentiation, namely professional specialization. Andrew Abbott's *The System of Professions* (Chicago: University of Chicago Press, 1988) provides a broad theoretical and comparative study of occupational differentiation and jurisdictional disputes among competing occupations. As valuable as these studies are, the actual organization of work within hospitals has been neglected. A similar criticism is made by Anselm Strauss et al., *Social Organization of Medical Work* (Chicago: University of Chicago Press, 1985), xi.
11. See Eliot Freidson, "Professions and the Occupational Principle," in *The Professions and their Prospects,* ed. Eliot Freidson (Beverly Hills: Sage, 1973), 19-38.
12. On physicians' professional dominance of nurses, see Eliot Freidson, *Profession of Medicine* (New York: Dodd, Mead and Co., 1970; Chicago: University of Chicago Press, 1988), chap. 3. On bureaucratic domination, see Etzioni, *Semi-Professions and their Organization,* v-xvii.
13. See Marie Manthey, *The Practice of Primary Nursing* (Boston: Blackwell Scientific Publications, 1980), chap. 1; Carl Joiner and Gwen Marram van Servellen, *Job Enrichment in Nursing* (Rockville, Md.: Aspen, 1984), chap. 2 and 3.

14. Harry Braverman, *Labor and Monopoly Capital* (New York: Monthly Review Press, 1974). For larger discussions of the literature on professional decline, see Charles Derber, "The Proletarianization of the Professional: A Review Essay," in *Professionals as Workers,* ed. Charles Derber (Boston: G. K. Hall, 1982), 13-34; Eliot Freidson, *Professional Powers* (Chicago: University of Chicago Press, 1986), chap. 6.

15. Manthey, *Practice of Primary Nursing*; Joiner and van Servellen, *Job Enrichment in Nursing,* chap. 2 and 3.

16. I discuss primary nursing and prior forms of nursing labor thoroughly in later chapters.

17. For a recent discussion, see Abbott, *System of Professions.*

18. I discuss Hughes' interpretation in detail in chap. 4.

19. See Braverman, *Labor and Monopoly Capital.*

20. Irene H. Butter et al., "Gender Hierarchies in the Health Labor Force," *International Journal of Health Services* 17(1) (1987): 133-149.

PART ONE

Political Economy, Corporatization, and Subordinate Workers

CHAPTER 1

The Changing Political Economy of Health Care

To understand the reorganization of nursing labor in the 1970s and 1980s, it is necessary to appreciate the social and historical context in which this change occurred. In Chapter 1, I set the stage by tracing the development of the industry and the growing contradiction that has led to the present cost containment era. While I am primarily interested in changes in the post-World War II period, much of the institutional infrastructure of the health care industry was established before the Great Depression. The decade of the 1930s was a watershed followed by a sustained expansion of the industry in the postwar period. The first phase of that expansion was based on the development of private insurance and a social contract between capital and labor that raised wages and extended health care benefits to American workers. The second phase added Medicare and Medicaid programs, and the health care industry continued to grow throughout the 1970s and 1980s. However, that growth was increasingly in contradiction with developments in the larger political economy. The cost of health care continued to rise at the same time that the larger economy entered a phase of declining profits, expanding debt, and tighter budgets. Corporations and the state then took action to contain health care expenditures, breaking the social contract between capital and labor and pressuring hospitals to contain the cost of producing services.

HEALTH CARE EXPANSION:
A GROWING CONTRADICTION

Between the last decades of the nineteenth century and the early decades of the twentieth century, health care was transformed from unpaid services produced by women in their households to service commodities produced by physicians and nurses. The establishment of the nation's hospitals was at the center of this change. From a small base of less than 180 hospitals in the early 1870s, the number of institutions grew to roughly 2000 by 1900 and to over 6800 by the late 1920s [1].

These institutions were established as the United States was transformed by industrialization, urbanization, and the development of capitalist corporations that increasingly dominated the society. Because hospitals were organized within a capitalist political economy, they were affected by its commercial ethos as well as by characteristically American constraints on the development of a public system for the provision of health care services. Public (state) hospitals originated with the nineteenth-century almshouse and remained associated with the care of the poor. Some hospitals were organized on a for-profit basis, while nonprofit community hospitals were established through the voluntary initiatives of citizens and groups, serving public needs through private means. Although voluntary hospitals were considered charitable institutions, they were also commercial businesses that charged patients for their services [2].

Nevertheless, private hospitals (both for-profit and nonprofit) remained distinct from capitalist corporations, or at least the large capitalist corporations. For-profit hospitals were small institutions established by physicians mostly in the more rural South and West in communities where other means for establishing a facility were unavailable. The majority of hospitals were nonprofit institutions established through community fund drives and capital derived from philanthropy, creating class alliances between physicians and the wealthy. Rather than gain a monetary return on their investment, the wealthy enjoyed the prestige accorded to public benefactors, and physicians and hospital authorities derived needed capital and the sponsorship of community elites. Once hospitals were established, philanthropic contributions met only a portion of operating expenses, so hospitals charged patients for their services. Still, unlike capitalist corporations, they were not in the business of generating a profit for capitalist owners or stockholders [3].

Hospitals were also unique in that as they developed, they combined bureaucratic and professional authority with institutional paternalism. Unlike the single authority structure characteristic of capitalist corporations, both physicians and hospital superintendents shared in the governance of hospitals. In addition, rather than manifest principles of capitalist rationality, hospitals were still largely paternalistic institutions. The nineteenth-century hospital had served the indigent, who sometimes stayed on to work in the hospital for room and board. When training schools for nurses were widely established in the first two decades of this century, newly established hospitals staffed with the unpaid labor of apprenticed nurses, who were required to live within the institution under the strict authority of hospital and nursing superintendents [4].

Despite these institutional restraints on corporate rationalization, by 1930 nonprofit or voluntary hospitals were already the central institutions of a major industry whose revenues accounted for 3.5 percent of Gross National Product (GNP) [5]. The financial infrastructure of the industry was vulnerable however, as the bulk of national health care expenditures was derived from income and wages. New technologies were already increasing the costs of health care when the economy collapsed during the Great Depression. During the worst years of the depression, between 1929 and 1933, GNP fell 28 percent at the same time that unemployment increased to 25 percent of the labor force. The wages of workers fortunate enough to have jobs fell sharply, and the capacity of many Americans to purchase services was severely curtailed [6]. Without an adequate income, members of working class and lower middle class households were likely to postpone seeing a doctor and "a major illness spelled financial crisis for all but the most wealthy members of society" [7].

As the consumption of services declined, the health care industry ceased to grow, and hospital income plummeted [8]. Nevertheless, the crisis was a turning point, providing hospitals and physicians an opportunity to overcome financial constraints and to consolidate their power at the center of the industry. In response to declining revenues, hospitals created their own solution by developing insurance programs under hospital and physician control. According to White, extensive debate about private health insurance occurred, with little result, until "hospitals in the private sector began to have problems with falling occupancy rates and bad debts." Hospitals then responded by developing "their own system of hospital insurance, Blue Cross, in an effort to bolster demand and reduce their losses from nonpayment" [9]. By 1940,

Blue Cross plans were serving over six million people and Blue Shield would soon be developed to guarantee the payment of physicians' fees [10]. Although capitalist insurance companies would increasingly compete with Blue Cross and Blue Shield for a larger share of the market, the financial infrastructure of the industry was now stabilized under private control, and as the economy re-expanded, rising costs would be passed on through insurance premiums.

Of course the reexpansion of the industry was dependent not only upon the development of health care insurance programs but on improvements in the economy. By 1940, both GNP and national health care expenditures had regained the levels reached before the crash. Unemployment remained high, but it was significantly below the worst years of the depression, and with the expansionary effect of war production, it dropped quickly thereafter [11].

To understand recent changes, it is useful to consider the postwar expansion of the health care industry in two phases. The first phase occurred between 1940 and 1965, during what is now recognized as one of the great boom periods of U.S. and international capitalism. As the economy expanded, so did the health care industry. During this period national health expenditures increased from four to forty-two billion dollars or from 4 to 6.1 percent of GNP [12]. Rising employment and wages enabled workers to purchase health care services and a variety of other goods and services they could not afford in the 1930s. However, with the growing costs of hospital services, the extension of health insurance coverage was of particular importance to the future growth of the industry.

During this period, a postwar accord and social contract between capital and labor created a privatized system of employer-based benefits that enabled more workers to purchase medical services. The extension of health insurance coverage and other employee benefits in the 1950s and 1960s set a standard for employment that ensured the continued expansion of the health care industry. As the economy grew, the vast majority of unionized workers were able to attain coverage and the gains of organized labor were extended to nonunion workers as well, often in a calculating manner by employers trying to keep the "union virus from infecting their employees" [13].

The second phase of expansion began in 1965 when state programs contributed an additional source of revenue to providers. With health care benefits linked to private employment, Medicare and Medicaid limited state-sponsored coverage to citizens excluded from or marginally connected with the employment system. Nevertheless, the

infusion of state subsidies contributed to the further growth and commodification of health care services. According to Brown, after 1965,
state expenditures "helped fuel inflation in medical costs by dumping
new funds into a privately controlled system ready to absorb every
penny into expansion, technology, high salaries, and profits" [14].
Health care was rapidly becoming a medical-industrial complex, and
large capitalist corporations moved from a concentration in insurance,
technology, and pharmaceuticals to organize a new sector of hospital
corporations. In contrast to the for-profit hospitals established earlier
in this century, such giants as the Hospital Corporation of America,
Humana, and American Medical International were multiple hospital
chains concerned specifically with profitability and a return on investment. While the majority of hospitals remained legally and nominally
nonprofit institutions, they were also commercial businesses determined to compete in the medical marketplace. Hospitals benefitted
greatly from state subsidies, particularly the Medicare program, in
which they were virtually allowed free rein in determining their own
costs and consequently the level of their reimbursement [15].

However, soon after the second phase of health care expansion
began, the larger economy entered a period of contraction. In 1974
Americans experienced a severe economic recession that marked the
close of the postwar period of affluence. During the 1970s and 1980s,
the economy seemed to fall apart. International financial arrangements became fragile and competing capitalist nations were able to
enter markets previously dominated by the United States. In the
United States, profitability, productivity, and real wages declined at
the same time that unemployment and inflation rose, prompting the
use of the term "stagflation" to describe conditions in the late 1970s.
Inflation declined in the 1980s, but only after the country experienced
another severe recession in 1981-82. Meanwhile, investment in new
productive capacity remained low and private capital engaged in a
wave of mergers and acquisitions. The economic recovery of the 1980s
was based on a rapid expansion of corporate, state, and consumer debt,
and by the end of the decade the economy was again in recession. Debt,
the savings and loan crisis, instability in the stock market, and greater
social inequality curbed the prospects for a new prosperity comparable
to that of earlier postwar decades. Americans were worried that their
children would no longer benefit by a rising standard of living [16].

At the same time that the larger economy was contracting, the
health care industry continued to expand, creating a growing contradiction manifested in the health care cost crisis. Between 1965 and

1984, national health care expenditures increased from 42 to 387 billion dollars or from 6.1 to 10.6 percent of GNP [17]. Health care had become "the quintessential industry of America's 'second industrial revolution,'" replacing the preeminence of the automobile industry as the nation shifted to services production [18]. Yet there is an important difference between the health care industry and capitalist industry generally, in that health care both contributes to and hinders capitalist accumulation. Health care expansion facilitates accumulation in the larger economy by providing new markets for business and employing workers no longer needed in other industries. However, health care is also a cost to non-health care corporations and the state [19].

With declining profits and fiscal constraints, both non-health care corporations and the state found it more difficult to absorb mushrooming health care costs. In the first phase of postwar expansion, health insurance premiums as a percentage of corporate profits before taxes increased from 6 percent in 1950 to 15 percent in 1965 [20]. Because the economy was expanding rapidly, corporations absorbed these costs and passed them on to consumers. However, by the end of the 1970s, corporations were spending sixty-five billion annually to maintain employee health care benefits, a cost that now amounted to 40 percent of corporate profits before taxes. The situation continued to worsen in the 1980s. By 1985, health care benefit costs had increased to 100 billion annually or close to 50 percent of profits before taxes. Health care had overtaken pension plans as the most expensive component of employer-based benefits [21]. Furthermore, throughout the 1980s, the seriousness of the problem was partly obscured by an overall rate of inflation that concealed significantly higher increases in the health care component of the consumer price index. Worried business leaders and the *Wall Street Journal* labeled the discrepancy "two-tier inflation" [22].

Meanwhile, the state was experiencing similar problems. As theorists of the state pointed out, social programs were themselves contradictory, contributing to political stability by mediating social and class tensions at the same time that they contributed to the fiscal crisis of the state [23]. By the mid-1980s, the Medicare and Medicaid programs accounted for 40 percent of total health care expenditures and over 50 percent of hospital revenues, straining the budgets of both national and local governments [24]. The state acts in a variety of ways to maintain accumulation [25] and with the growing crisis of rising health care costs, both the state and non-health care corporations, particularly large corporations in the monopoly sector, were forced to intervene in the health care marketplace.

CAPITAL AND STATE RESPONSE TO RISING HEALTH CARE COSTS

As capitalist accumulation slowed and the health care industry continued to expand, employers and the state mounted efforts to control health care costs. These efforts can be grouped into two general strategies. First, employers shifted a greater burden of rising costs onto workers, an approach that was part of a larger corporate offensive that broke the postwar social contract between capital and labor in an effort to increase profitability and reduce total labor costs. Second, corporate purchasers and the state increasingly pressured health care providers to contain their costs. This strategy included a variety of means, from the greater participation of corporations in formulating health care policy to the development of alternative provider organizations and major changes in reimbursement.

Breaking the Social Contract

Davis has argued that the postwar labor accord was always contingent and more of a truce than a social contract [26]. Similarly, Bluestone and Harrison maintain that

> the extent to which capital as a class deliberately and consciously *decided* to call a cease-fire with organized labor . . . can be exaggerated. Managers might more accurately be described as having grudgingly accepted the collective bargaining process, considering the apparent benefits that union cooperation in the management of stable industrial relations gave to them [27].

In any case the

> social contract with organized labor in particular and the extension of the social wage in general were clearly predicated on more or less continuous economic growth. . . . As the conditions underlying that growth fell apart . . . , it was inevitable that both the willingness of capital to honor the social contract and the ability of the U.S. economy to afford a large and growing social safety net would come to an end [27].

In the 1970s and 1980s, many workers fell through the social safety net when corporations in major manufacturing industries shifted production elsewhere or invested in businesses with a higher rate of return. With de-industrialization and capital mobility, corporations moved their production facilities to geographical areas in both the domestic and international economy where wages and benefits were lower, and where workers were less likely to be under union contract. As plants closed, communities of unemployed and underemployed workers were left behind. Job loss in core industries typically resulted not only in the loss of direct wages, but also health care benefits and other components of the social wage that had been attained through employer-based programs. As a result, the number of citizens without health insurance increased from twenty-nine million in 1979 to thirty-seven million in 1986. The majority of the dispossessed were the working poor who had suffered job displacement [28].

In the absence of national health insurance or a national health program, corporations continuing production in the United States could not simply eliminate their benefit programs, but what they could do was shift rising benefit costs onto their employees. While the postwar social contract had guaranteed wage and benefit improvements in successive rounds of collective bargaining, now workers were confronted by corporate demands for concessions. The corporate concessions campaign began largely with the bailout of the Chrysler Corporation in the 1970s through employee "givebacks." "Collective bargaining in reverse" then spread through all the major industries in the 1980s, becoming a generalized strategy for cutting labor costs and weakening union contracts in both financially vulnerable and profitable companies alike. In the early years of this campaign, union resistance as well as concessions in direct wages and other benefits buffered workers from corporate demands for concessions on health care benefits. However, as costs continued to rise, companies increased their efforts to gain concessions on these benefits as well. Such demands became a major strike issue during the 1980s, but unions were on the defensive while business had the advantage of state administrations openly supportive of business interests [29].

Consequently, corporations succeeded in shifting costs onto employees by increasing their insurance deductibles and copayments for services. A survey of 250 of the nation's largest corporations reported that companies requiring employees to pay deductibles increased from 14 percent in 1979 to a majority of 52 percent by the mid-1980s [30]. The trend continued and because unions were unable to maintain prior levels of coverage, the benefits of nonunion workers were reduced as well. As a result, both union and nonunion workers alike pay a greater proportion of their health care benefits from direct wages.

Pressuring Health Care Providers to Control Costs

In addition to breaking the postwar social contract and shifting rising costs onto employees, capital and the state initiated programs to pressure hospitals and physicians to contain the costs of producing services. Such initiatives began in the early 1970s but became more threatening to providers in the late 1970s and in the 1980s.

While non-health care corporations were reluctant to attack capitalist corporations profiting in the production and sale of health care goods and services, they may also have been reluctant to attack nonprofit hospitals governed by middle class managers and physicians. As Wright has argued, "dominant exploiting classes have generally pursued class alliances" with the middle class "when they were financially capable of doing so." Such alliances link the interests of managers and professionals to the "dominant exploiting class," and help contain struggles by exploited classes [31]. Davis has suggested that the continued expansion of the health care industry during the 1970s and 1980s was due to such an alliance. Rather than threaten the share of the surplus flowing to middle class managers and professionals, capital attempted to maintain an alliance while shifting costs onto workers and the poor [32].

As I have indicated, shifting costs onto workers was certainly a part of the corporate response. Nevertheless, with the intractability of the cost crisis, and because workers can absorb only a fraction of these costs, capital and the state were forced to pressure hospitals and physicians. Class alliances can be expensive when the larger economy is experiencing stagnation or decline, and when middle class managers and professionals are allowed "access to significant portions of the social surplus" [33]. Although non-health care corporations and the state did not move to destroy social arrangements that allowed private interests to profit in the health care industry, they did pressure providers to control their costs. Corporations were able to do so by increasing their participation in health care policy and by creating or promoting organizational reforms and alternatives.

Beginning in the early 1970s, non-health care corporations attempted to influence health care policy through the formation and activities of various business groups. The Washington Business Group on Health (WBGH) was one of the most influential groups at the national level. According to Willis B. Goldbeck,

> somewhere in the early 1970s a few business leaders began to notice a number of problems which, today, we know are inter-related. The productivity of the average worker was declining. [However,] the utilization and the cost of medical benefits was going up—fast [34].

In response to the detrimental effect of rising health care costs, the WBGH was established in 1974 by the Business Roundtable, a major policy and advocacy organization for Fortune 500 companies. The WBGH was to focus solely on the health care cost crisis and to provide an organizational means of formulating corporate policy positions and communicating them to state elites and health care providers [35].

Other business groups and coalitions were also organized, and at the national, state, and local levels. Throughout the 1970s and 1980s, the Conference Board published studies on rising costs and was credited with calling the first national conference of corporate execu-tives and representatives of the health care industry to address the problem [36]. The conservative American Enterprise Institute pub-lished numerous studies in health policy, and held a national con-ference in Washington attended by elites from business, government, and the health care industry, including representatives from the American Hospital Association, Blue Cross, and the American Medical Association [37]. At the regional level, Bergthold argues that alliances between business and government elites were instrumental in counter-ing the power of health care providers. Meanwhile, close to 200 busi-ness and health coalitions formed in localities throughout the United States to educate members, influence policy, and pressure providers to contain their costs [38].

Corporations themselves developed a variety of strategies to control costs or develop organizational alternatives they hoped would do so. Companies pressured insurance intermediaries to tighten their reim-bursement policies, and insurance companies, in turn, implemented new rules that threatened providers with a loss of income and/or consumers with greater out of pocket expense if they did not comply with new restrictions in their insurance policies. Employers also modified their benefit plans to include incentives for outpatient treat-ment, which was believed to be less expensive than hospitalization. In some cases, employers even took over the role of the insurance inter-mediary by providing their own corporate insurance [39]. Ironically, at the same time that employers reduced expenditures by shifting a greater burden of costs onto their employees, they invested in new company-based "wellness" programs they hoped would contribute to reducing their medical costs. Corporate wellness programs grew rapidly in the 1980s, ranging from company gymnasiums and fitness programs to health education classes and counseling services. Programs were more extensive at Fortune 500 companies, with International Business Machines and Rockwell International leading the field. Still, approximately 50 percent of companies with more than fifty employees offered some kind of program [40].

In one of the most important developments, corporations and the state promoted alternative provider organizations and the "managed care" approach. There were several variants, but all involved changing the financial incentive of providers. Health maintenance organizations (HMOs) combined insurance and health care delivery within a single organization. As pre-paid, fixed-rate providers, HMOs have an incentive to withhold services, as the size of their surplus is dependent upon providing services under the fixed rates charged for enrollment. Corporations contracted with HMOs such as Kaiser or started their own HMO. Organizational variants of the managed care approach included preferred provider organizations or PPOs, which contract with employers and third-party payors to provide services at discounted rates [41].

In addition to promoting alternative provider organizations, the state increased its efforts to contain the costs of Medicare and Medicaid. A decade of regulatory programs during the 1970s led to the realization that such efforts were usually compromised by the interests of providers. Peer review and professional standards review organizations relied on the voluntary efforts of physicians and hospitals. The effectiveness of health system agencies (HSAs), established to control the expansion of hospital plant and technology by issuing "certificates of need," was often constrained by the politics and interests of local agency members and the power of providers [42]. Consequently, as costs continued to rise in the 1980s, the state finally moved to tighten reimbursement in public programs. In 1983, Congress passed amendments to the Social Security Act that established a prospective payment system (PPS) by diagnostically related groups or DRGs. Beginning in 1984, hospitals were reimbursed a predetermined, fixed amount for each diagnostic category, reversing the retrospective reimbursement system that had been part of Medicare since 1965. Meanwhile, the federal government also shifted a greater burden of Medicaid costs onto the states, forcing regional authorities to reform their programs. Many states were experiencing their own fiscal crises, and with tighter reimbursement, providers found the cost of treating Medicaid patients could exceed reimbursement. Private community hospitals were accused of dumping inadequately insured patients onto public hospitals, institutions already burdened with caring for the destitute [43].

Threatened by tighter reimbursement and greater competition, community hospitals sought a course of action which would secure their position in the industry. Their response would alter the organizational structure and culture of voluntary, nonprofit hospitals and have a significant effect on those working to produce patient care within them.

NOTES

1. George Rosen, *The Structure of American Medical Practice: 1875-1941,* ed. Charles E. Rosenberg (Philadelphia: University of Pennsylvania Press, 1983), 23, 46; Paul Starr, *The Social Transformation of American Medicine* (New York: Basic Books), 73.
2. For social histories of the hospital and health care in American society, see Starr, *Social Transformation of American Medicine*; Richard E. Brown, *Rockefeller Medicine Men: Medicine and Capitalism in America* (Berkeley: University of California Press, 1979); Charles E. Rosenberg, *The Care of Strangers: The Rise of America's Hospital System* (New York: Basic Books, 1987); Rosemary Stevens, *In Sickness and in Wealth* (New Haven: Basic Books, 1989).
3. For discussions of relations between physicians and elites, see Brown, *Rockefeller Medicine Men*; Starr, *Social Transformation of American Medicine,* 153. Useful comparative data on for-profit, voluntary, and public sector hospitals is presented in J. Rogers Hollingsworth and Ellen Jane Hollingsworth, *Controversy about American Hospitals: Funding, Ownership, and Performance* (Washington: American Enterprise Institute for Public Policy Research, 1987). For a discussion of the centrality of the voluntary sector, see Stevens, *In Sickness and in Wealth.*
4. For discussions of the bureaucratic and paternalistic features of hospitals, see Jo Ann Ashley, *Hospitals, Paternalism, and the Role of the Nurse* (New York: Teachers College Press, 1976); Susan M. Reverby, *Ordered to Care* (Cambridge: Cambridge University Press, 1987); Rosenberg, *Care of Strangers*; Karen Brodkin Sacks, *Caring by the Hour* (Urbana: University of Illinois Press, 1988); Starr, *Social Transformation of American Medicine.* I discuss the hospital apprenticeship system in detail in chap. 3.
5. National Center for Health Statistics, *Health: United States, 1985* (Hyattsville, Md.: Public Health Service, 1986), table 80.
6. David Milton, *The Politics of U.S. Labor: From the Great Depression to the New Deal* (New York: Monthly Review Press, 1982), 25; Irving Bernstein,

A Caring Society: The New Deal, the Worker, and the Great Depression (Boston: Houghton Mifflin, 1985), 277-278.

7. William D. White, "The American Hospital Industry Since 1900," in *Advances in Health Economics and Health Services Research,* ed. Richard M. Scheffler and Louis F. Rossiter (Greenwich, Conn.: JAI Press, 1982), vol. 3, p. 159.

8. Starr, *Social Transformation of American Medicine,* 295.

9. White, "American Hospital Industry," 161.

10. Starr, *Social Transformation of American Medicine,* 298.

11. Bernstein, *Caring Society,* table, p. 277. For data on national health care expenditures and GNP, see National Center for Health Statistics, *Health: United States, 1985,* table 80.

12. National Center for Health Statistics, *Health: United States, 1985,* table 80. For a discussion of the postwar expansion of the economy, see David M. Gordon, Richard Edwards, and Michael Reich, *Segmented Work, Divided Workers* (Cambridge: Cambridge University Press, 1982).

13. Robert H. Zieger, *American Workers, American Unions, 1920-1985* (Baltimore: Johns Hopkins University Press, 1986), 153. For additional discussion of the gains of organized labor in the postwar period, see David Brody, *Workers in Industrial America: Essays on the 20th Century Struggle* (New York: Oxford University Press, 1980) and Nelson Lichtenstein, *Labor's War at Home: The CIO in World War II* (Cambridge: Cambridge University Press, 1982). For discussions of the postwar social contract, see Samuel Bowles and Herbert Gintis, "The Crisis of Liberal Democratic Capitalism: The Case of the United States," *Politics and Society* 11(1) (1982): 51-94; Richard Edwards and Michael Podgursky, "The Unraveling Accord: American Unions in Crisis" in *Unions in Crisis and Beyond,* ed. Richard Edwards, Paolo Garonna, and Franz Todtling (Dover, Mass.: Auburn House, 1986), 14-60.

14. Brown, *Rockefeller Medicine Men,* 2.

15. For a discussion of the medical-industrial complex, see Barbara and John Ehrenreich, *The American Health Empire: Power, Profits, and Politics* (New York: Random House, 1970). On the growth of for-profit hospital corporations, see Starr, *Social Transformation of American Medicine,* book 2, chapter 5. For additional discussion of the nonprofit institutions, see Thomas A. Barocci, *Non-Profit Hospitals* (Boston: Auburn House, 1981).

16. On the postwar economic contraction and its social consequences, see Paul Blumberg, *Inequality in an Age of Decline* (New York: Oxford University Press, 1980); Gordon, Edwards, and Reich, *Segmented Work, Divided Workers;* Ernest Mandel, *Late Capitalism* (London: Verso, 1975). On economic conditions in the 1980s, see Paul Sweezy and Harry Magdoff, "The Logic of Stagnation," *Monthly Review* 38(5) (Oct. 1986): 1-19.

17. National Center for Health Statistics, *Health: United States, 1985,* table 80.

18. Sacks, *Caring by the Hour,* 24.

19. For discussions of the contradictions between health care expansion and accumulation in the larger economy, see Leonard Rodberg and Gelvin Stevenson, "The Health Care Industry in Advanced Capitalism," *Review of Radical Political Economy* 8 (Spring 1977): 104-115; J. Warren Salmon, "Monopoly Capital and the Reorganization of the Health Sector," *Review of Radical Political Economy* 8 (Spring 1977): 125-133; David U. Himmelstein and Steffie Woolhandler, "Medicine as Industry: The Health-Care Sector in the United States," *Monthly Review* 35(11) (Apr. 1984): 13-25; Himmelstein and Woolhandler, "The Corporate Compromise," *Monthly Review* 42(1) (May 1990): 14-29.

20. Victor R. Fuchs, *The Health Economy* (Cambridge, Mass.: Harvard University Press, 1986), table 17.2.

21. Additional data on rising health care costs from Himmelstein and Woolhandler, "Medicine as Industry," 20; *New York Times,* 3 Mar. 1985, p. 11; Sanford C. Bernstein and Co., *The Future of Health Care Delivery in America* (privately published, 1985), 43; "Health Care Fast Becoming the Costliest Benefit," *Employee Benefit Plan Review,* 38(12) (June 1984): 104-106.

22. *Wall Street Journal,* 11 Sept. 1986, p. 1.

23. For a larger discussion of the crisis and politics of the state, see James O'Connor, *The Fiscal Crisis of the State* (New York: St. Martin's Press, 1973); Bowles and Gintis, "Crisis of Liberal Democratic Capitalism," 51-94.

24. National Center for Health Statistics, *Health: United States, 1985,* table 87; Gerald F. Anderson, "National Medical Care Spending," *Health Affairs* (Fall 1986), exhibit 2, p. 124.

25. For theoretical discussions of the role of the state in maintaining accumulation, including containing conflict and legitimizing social arrangements, see Mandel, *Late Capitalism*; Vicente Navarro, *Medicine Under Capitalism* (New York: Prodist, 1976), Part IV; Claus Offe, *Contradictions of the Welfare State* (Cambridge: MIT Press, 1985).

26. Mike Davis, *Prisoners of the American Dream* (London: Verso, 1986), chap. 3.

27. Barry Bluestone and Bennett Harrison, *The Deindustrialization of America: Plant Closings, Community Abandonment, and the Dismantling of Basic Industry* (New York: Basic Books, 1982), 139.

28. For a discussion of the effects of deindustrialization on workers, see Bluestone and Harrison, *Deindustrialization of America,* chap. 3. For data on the uninsured, see *Wall Street Journal,* 3 June 1986, p. 60; *New York Times,* 21 Nov. 1982, E4; 13 Jan. 1987, p. 1.

29. For discussion of these issues, see Davis, *Prisoners of the American Dream,* chap. 3; Kim Moody, *An Injury to All* (London: Verso, 1988), chap. 8; Jane Slaughter, *Concessions* (Detroit: Labor Education and Research Project, 1983).

30. The survey was conducted by Hewitt Associates and reported in the *New York Times,* 3 Mar. 1985, p. 11. Another private survey by Mercer-Meidinger, Inc. of 900 chief executive officers of "the nation's largest industrial and service companies," found that a majority of executives believed "the United States is facing a health care cost crisis." Executives acknowledged that a principal means of cost control was to shift rising costs onto their workers, indicating that in the future employees would be paying "a 'substantially' higher portion of health-benefit plan costs." They also acknowledged the growing inequality that was likely to result as "high costs and limited access to high-tech medical care will create a two-tier medical care system in the United States: one for the rich and one for the poor." Quotations are from survey results reported in *Compensation and Benefit Review* (Nov.-Dec. 1985): 7.

31. Erik Olin Wright, "What is Middle About the Middle Class?" in *Analytical Marxism,* ed. John Roemer (Cambridge: Cambridge University Press, 1986), 130.

32. Davis, *Prisoners of the American Dream,* 219.

33. Wright, "What is Middle About the Middle Class?" 130.

34. Willis B. Goldbeck, *A Business Perspective on Industry and Health Care,* vol. 2 in Springer Series on Industry and Health Care (New York: Springer-Verlag, 1978), 10.

35. For further discussion of the WBGH and other business groups, see Linda A. Bergthold, *Purchasing Power in Health* (New Brunswick: Rutgers University Press, 1990); Betty Leyerle, *Moving and Shaking American Medicine* (Westport, Conn.: Greenwood Press, 1984).

36. Leyerle, *Moving and Shaking American Medicine,* 10.

37. Sean Sullivan, *Managing Health Care Costs* (Washington: American Enterprise Institute, 1984).

38. Bergthold, *Purchasing Power in Health,* 51.

39. Various strategies are discussed in Leyerle, *Moving and Shaking American Medicine* and in the Springer Series on Industry and Health Care, including Richard H. Egdahl and Diana Chapman Walsh, eds., *Containing Health Benefit Costs* (New York: Springer-Verlag, 1979), vol. 6.

40. *New York Times,* 5 Oct. 1986, F19.

41. For a discussion of the development of HMOs and other forms of managed care, see Leyerle, *Moving and Shaking American Medicine,* chap. 4.

42. Ibid., chap. 5.

43. For discussions of regulatory efforts and reforms, see Bergthold, *Purchasing Power in Health*; Eli Ginzberg, *The Medical Triangle* (Cambridge, Mass.: Harvard University Press, 1990); Leyerle, *Moving and Shaking American Medicine*; Mary Ruggie, "The Paradox of Liberal Intervention: Health Policy and the American Welfare State," *American Journal of Sociology* 97 (4) (1992): 919-944.

CHAPTER 2

Corporatization and the Reorganization of Community Hospitals

Community hospitals responded to the changing political economy of the industry by reorganizing for survival and continued business expansion. In doing so, they took on many of the characteristics of capitalist corporations. In this chapter corporatization and its effects both on the governance of voluntary, nonprofit hospitals and on subordinate production workers are discussed. As managerial hierarchies and functions grew, the governing tripartite was altered, expanding the power of corporate managers and threatening that of trustees and physicians. In addition, as hospitals restructured, corporate managers mounted efforts to contain labor costs and increase productivity, reorganizing work and taking a more aggressive posture in collective bargaining. I include material from my case study at Pacific Hospital to support arguments regarding corporatization, the restructuring of power among hospital elites, and new managerial strategies toward subordinate production workers.

HOSPITALS REORGANIZE FOR CONTINUED BUSINESS EXPANSION

Throughout the 1970s and into the 1980s, the corporatization of hospitals was associated largely with the growth of for-profit hospital corporations. During this period, the Hospital Corporation of America became the largest of the for-profit chains, expanding from the owner-ship or control of 23 hospitals in 1970 to more than 300 by 1981 [1]. With the growth of these chains, experts expected that the ownership of hospitals might undergo significant changes. Some suggested that the voluntary, nonprofit sector might even be subsumed by capitalist hospital corporations. Experts debated the relative costs and efficien-cies of for-profit versus nonprofit systems as well as the ethical implica-tions of privatizing services. All seemed to agree that corporatization was transforming American medicine, and the most visible indication was the growth of the for-profit hospital corporations that were intro-ducing managerial capitalism and rationality into the production of health care services [2].

By the end of the 1980s it was clear that the corporatization of the industry had not taken place simply or even primarily through the growth of capitalist hospital corporations, but rather through the reor-ganization of voluntary, nonprofit hospitals [3]. Threatened by pres-sures from non-health care capital and the state as well as by increased competition from for-profit hospital chains and HMOs, community hospitals responded by adapting organizational forms and managerial strategies used by capitalist corporations, a classic case of what DiMaggio and Powell refer to as "institutional isomorphism" [4].

The corporatization of community hospitals is well documented and includes a variety of features and adaptations. The major strategies include diversification into new businesses, the adaptation of holding company models that preserve the tax-exempt status of hospitals at the same time that the parent organization invests in for-profit sub-sidiaries, and the adoption of more rationalized systems of manage-ment. The process by which community hospitals reorganized into diversified and integrated health care corporations often began with vertical integration as hospitals launched businesses at other levels of care. Establishing nursing homes and home health care agencies enabled hospitals to discharge patients to corporate facilities that cap-tured additional income and served to channel patients into the hos-pital. Furthermore, as cost containment targeted hospitals, services that could be organized on an outpatient basis or in clinics and laboratories were developed as subsidiary businesses, many of them for profit. Hospitals also integrated horizontally by developing a variety of new business arrangements that included contractual agreements with other hospitals, joint ventures, affiliations, and out-right mergers into multiple hospital systems. Management agreements coordinated services among individual hospitals, joint ventures and affiliations pooled resources, and mergers centralized management and corporate assets [5].

To control a variety of subsidiary businesses, hospitals reorganized into corporate forms that allowed them to include both nonprofit hospitals and diversified for-profit and nonprofit subsidiaries under the same umbrella. The most important organizational form was the corporate holding company, which had been successfully used in capitalist finance to manage a variety of individual, operationally decentralized subsidiaries such as banks, savings and loans, investment brokerages, and insurance companies. In reorganizing nonprofit hospitals, administrators adapted variations of the holding company model to centralize control over the expansion of subsidiary businesses while protecting the nonprofit legal status of hospitals. Assets and income formerly shown on the hospital's financial statement could be transferred to the holding company, and the hospital could then show a lower level of equity and revenues [6]. By doing so, reorganized hospitals could reduce the visibility of diverse business operations to the public and to regulators. According to one expert,

> the corporate reorganization enabled the hospital to minimize the exposure of confidential information to the regulators, to its competitors, to the press, and to community agitators and activists. Income and assets that were formerly reported are now safely tucked away in the financial statements of non-hospital corporations. Since accounting principles only require vertical financial consolidation, the only place all financial activity is reported is on the financial statements of the parent corporation. Regulatory agencies have no authority to receive these financial statements [7].

To successfully implement such strategies, hospital authorities consulted with accounting and legal firms that for a sizeable fee provided the technical expertise.

Hospitals also adopted more rationalized systems of management to effectively determine costs and increase profit margins when possible, an organizational process that became critical with tighter reimbursement. Managers adapted concepts like "product line management" from capitalist industry, subordinating production and marketing decisions to the profitability of each "service line" [8]. Service line managers attempted to both reduce production costs and employ more sophisticated marketing strategies to expand profitable services. Health care corporations that used such methods were more likely to turn the prospective payment system into a profitable means of reimbursement, often attempting "to beat the DRG/PPS system" by "choosing the principal diagnosis or procedure carefully" to maximize reimbursement [9]. Because hospitals suffered a loss if the cost of treatment exceeded Medicare reimbursement, it was "in their interest to be selective about the patients they admit[ted], scrutinize tests and procedures, discharge patients as soon as possible, and encourage greater use of outpatient services," where costs were lower but where charges were less subject to external control [10].

Although other factors were certainly involved, because many hospitals were able to reorganize and adapt successfully to capital and state cost control programs, health care expenditures continued to grow. Of course, not all hospitals realized gains, and those that did profited unevenly. The more successful had planned well and were likely to be financially better off to begin with [11].

Illustration from a Leading Hospital: Pacific Hospital Reorganizes into Pacific Health Care Corporation

In the late 1970s and early 1980s, several hundred hospitals led the industry in reorganizing to expand and diversify their revenues as capital and the state increased their efforts to slow accumulation among health care providers [12]. Pacific Hospital was among these leaders and was formally recognized in the industry as a model for corporatization.

When I began working at Pacific Hospital in 1979, the organization was still a single institution, although it no longer resembled the eight bed sanatorium established by a nurse in a Victorian residence near the turn of the century [13]. A hospital with over 100 beds was built in the late 1920s, a new building was added in the 1950s, and further construction in the 1960s and 1970s resulted in an acute-care hospital with over 300 beds, serving an urban community within the San Francisco Bay area. Within ten miles of the hospital were several other hospitals of similar size serving contiguous communities and some of the same client population [14].

Initially Pacific Hospital was a for-profit hospital, which, as I indicated earlier, was not uncommon among hospitals in the South and the West. Revenues and assets increased substantially after World War II when the hospital shifted to a nonprofit status to take advantage of tax exemptions and state subsidies. While the facilities expanded throughout the postwar period, the hospital remained a free-standing institution that derived its entire revenue from acute care services.

When corporate and state cost containment pressures began in the early 1970s, Pacific Hospital began to diversify by acquiring nursing homes and establishing a foundation for fund-raising that community activists argued served to shelter revenues from the newly acquired nursing homes. In the mid-1970s, hospital administrators developed a strategic plan to reorganize the hospital into a regional health care corporation. The plan was implemented over the next decade, and during my employment, Pacific rapidly diversified into a polycorporate system of subsidiary nonprofit and for-profit companies.

As Pacific Hospital reorganized into Pacific Health Care Corporation, a parent holding company with the financial and regulatory advantages discussed earlier, the hospital itself became a subsidiary of Pacific Hospital Affiliates, a divisional holding company that was formed to administer what managers hoped would become a system of affiliated hospitals. During the next few years, the corporation pursued regional affiliations, leased other hospitals in the area, and started a company that contracted to manage hospitals. The acquisition of a nearby institution assured Pacific Hospital of a monopoly over local services. The corporation also started its own health maintenance organization that later changed from a nonprofit to a for-profit subsidiary, invested in a regional preferred provider organization (PPO), in real estate that included physician office buildings, and in a joint venture with other regional health care corporations to build a new medical center in a rapidly expanding business corridor in California.

Another divisional holding company, Pacific Ambulatory Health Services, directed a growing number of diversified businesses on the periphery of Pacific's hospitals. Because hospitals were targeted for cost containment, the corporation invested heavily in new businesses less subject to regulation and price constraints. By the late 1980s, Pacific Ambulatory Health Services' ownership of extensive for-profit and nonprofit subsidiaries included two laboratories, a home health agency, a hospice, a corporate health investment firm that provided services to business clients, a sports care clinic, a dialysis center, a clinic for the treatment of AIDS patients, a regional network of magnetic resonance imaging centers, over fifteen nursing homes, and several retirement centers.

The success of Pacific's corporatization was reflected in increased revenues during the very same years that the national health care cost crisis worsened. In 1974, the hospital's revenues and net-excess (the term for profit) of approximately one million dollars came entirely from inpatient services. Revenues increased during the 1970s as the hospital entered the nursing home business and established its foundation for fund raising. With further diversification, the corporation's annual surpluses grew to approximately $3.5 million in 1980 and to $7.1 million in 1981. In the next two years, corporate profits doubled again to $14 million. Pacific Hospital itself had historically high profits in these years. According to the 1983 annual report, the hospital reported a surplus of $6.9 million, which according to management represented "a 19 percent improvement over 1982 and a 151 percent improvement over 1981." Because the corporation was not owned by stockholders, presumably these surpluses were reinvested in further expansion and used to offset growing administrative overhead.

I was unable to confirm revenues and surpluses after 1983 because corporate management exercised greater confidentiality and did not issue annual reports available to the public or employees. However, the 1983 annual report projected continued profitability throughout the 1980s. Although the corporation's hospitals remained the largest source of revenues, profits were expected to flow increasingly from peripheral businesses. Thus, whereas 100 percent of profits originated at Pacific Hospital in 1974, only 56 percent did so in 1983, and by the end of the decade, management expected fully half of corporate profits to originate from diversified new businesses. Executives summarized the corporation's position in the new health care marketplace succinctly in the following statement contained in the 1983 annual report.

> [Pacific] has positioned itself to minimize the impact of long-term trends. With the combination of a successful diversification program, a strong capital structure, and a successful hospital contracting and marketing program, the [Pacific] family of companies is unusually well-positioned for the future.

If business expansion is an indication of its financial strength, corporatization and growth appeared to have protected Pacific from cost containment and increased competition, although its profit levels may have declined in the late 1980s. Pacific management monitored national trends closely and like other health care leaders was convinced that those restructured companies that gained regional control over the marketplace would be the companies best positioned for survival and continued expansion. Because of the success of health care corporations like Pacific, the *New York Times* reported in 1987 that hospitals across the country were following the example of such institutions [15].

CORPORATIZATION AND THE GOVERNING TRIPARTITE

As hospitals responded to external pressures through corporatization, power in the governing tripartite of these institutions shifted toward administrators, a restructuring that would have a significant effect not only upon elites but upon subordinate workers as well.

Unlike the relatively simple power structure in capitalist corporations, power in hospitals is complicated by the interlinking of administrative and professional authority as well as the participation of trustees. Internal changes in this governing tripartite are not new, for power shifts among administrators, physicians, and trustees have occurred at different phases of the industry's development. In the early 1960s, Perrow maintained that the dominant group within the tripartite was likely to vary according to which group's contribution is most critical to the attainment of organizational goals. Perrow argued that in the period from the late 19th century to the 1930s, during which the majority of hospitals were founded, trustees dominated the tripartite because physicians and administrators were dependent upon community elites for both capital and social legitimation. From the 1930s to the post-World War II period, physicians rose to dominance based on their control over the admission of patients and their critical role in the production of medical services. However, throughout the postwar period, the role of administrators grew in importance as hospitals and the health care environment were becoming more organizationally complex [16].

As community hospitals underwent corporatization in the 1970s and 1980s, adding new layers of management over what had previously been relatively small staffs headed by hospital administrators, overhead costs ballooned. By the mid-1980s administrative costs in the industry as a whole reached over 20 percent of national health care expenditures [17]. Presumably these costs included the salaries of health care executives, some of whom possessed credentials from business schools and experience in the for-profit sector. In competition with capitalist businesses for managerial expertise, restructured health care corporations rewarded corporate executives with high incomes and employment contracts that included perquisites such as company automobiles and club memberships [18].

The growth of administrative costs reflected the reorganization of the tripartite and the shift of power toward corporate managers. With corporatization and the greater complexity of newly restructured institutions, trustees and physicians became more dependent upon managers' business expertise, supporting Perrow's argument that the fraction of the tripartite that addresses "the distinctive problem the organization faces because of its stage of development," will tend to dominate [19]. In discussing the effects of corporatization on trustees' role, Rosemary Stevens states that "voluntary hospitals are no longer the amiable creatures of corporate capitalism, with business and religious representatives on their boards; they are also big businesses themselves. In this process, there has been a breakdown in the role of voluntary-hospital trustees as benevolent guardians of the larger capitalist ethos—and/or as the altruistic extension of this ethos. The very success of hospitals as entrepreneurial business organizations has called the role of trustees into question" [20].

The effect of corporatization on physicians is more complex. Because the health care system had been organized largely around the professional interests of medicine, discussions of the effects of corporatization have been preoccupied with the consequences for physicians' professional power. In 1970, when Freidson wrote of medicine's "professional dominance," physicians' power seemed quite secure [21]. A decade later Starr warned of the "coming of the corporation," and by the late 1980s, sociologists debated whether Freidson's analysis had actually marked the end of an era and the beginning of physicians' professional decline [22]. This possibility is of particular importance to my study as the work of physicians and nurses is interconnected. Furthermore, a major decline in physicians' power would suggest that physicians no longer participate effectively in the governance of hospitals and may be less likely to dominate nurses and subordinate hospital workers.

Clearly physicians have become more subject to external controls as non-health care capital and the state have organized to contain costs. As a result, physicians' power in the health care system seems to be declining, although Navarro questions whether physicians ever dominated the system itself [23]. Physicians also appear to be losing power at the institutional level. When subjected to managerial decisions, greater bureaucratic control and more rationalized organizational procedures that include tighter cost accounting systems, physicians may experience a relative loss of power and autonomy, what Ritzer and Walczak consider a deprofessionalization of the occupation [24]. In a more extreme view of professional decline, it is argued that physicians may be subject to proletarianization, suggesting a major reorganization of their work and the possibility of downward class mobility. McKinlay has argued that a vulnerability to employment and bureaucratic control may result in physicians being dominated and exploited by managers and perhaps even deskilled in a manner analogous to the deskilling of craft workers earlier in this century [25]. Other theorists sympathetic to the thesis of physicians' proletarianization have argued that doctors are unlikely to experience the degradation associated with the industrial proletariat. Derber has argued that the process will likely be limited to "ideological proletarianization," in which doctors lose control over the larger organizational setting and purposes of medical work, but that physicians are unlikely to experience "technical proletarianization," a loss of occupational control over their immediate work tasks [26].

The debate over the extent of physicians' professional decline is complicated by several considerations. Although physicians have been considered the epitome of successful professionalization, their independence from bureaucratic organization and employment has been exceptional rather than typical of the larger category of professional occupations. Thus, even if the majority of physicians become subject to managerial and bureaucratic authority, it is not clear that this would result in professional decline or proletarianization as much as a transition from autonomous to heteronomous professional organization [27]. Physicians would no doubt experience this transition as an attack on their professional power and autonomy, but like other professional occupations, they may also adapt to and modify formal bureaucracies while retaining control over their occupational jurisdiction and medical work. While heteronomous professional organizations are associated with semiprofessional occupations like nurses and teachers, other occupations, including university professors and scientists, provide examples of more successful professionalization within bureaucratic settings. Hence, the effects of employment may vary considerably. Work in bureaucratic settings can even increase the autonomy and power of professions when the alternative of self-employment requires participation in an unfavorable labor market or when clients have significant control over the occupation's work [28].

Although physicians may be vulnerable to deprofessionalization or proletarianization, rather than suffer absolute decline they may be subject to new forms of stratification in which some are more likely to experience greater bureaucratic control and less status and rewards than others. Physicians are more likely to be employed by bureaucratic organizations than in the past and the income of employee physicians is significantly less than those in private practice (self-employment) [29]. The greater organizational employment of physicians has resulted from a combination of factors including the growth of group practices and managed care HMOs, an oversupply of physicians in urban areas, and the difficulty that new graduates experience in establishing a private practice. Employee physicians are disproportionately young and/or female. Those employed in less desirable organizational settings, particularly medical staff HMOs or public hospitals, are more likely to experience dissatisfaction [30].

Furthermore, despite what seems to be a trend toward increased employment, the majority of physicians are not employed by hospitals and health care corporations, either capitalist or nonprofit. Most physicians continue in individual or group practice with admitting privileges at voluntary hospitals and to a lesser extent at for-profit corporations [31]. Although physicians working in group practices may be "employed," in actuality they are not wage labor as these physicians are on salary in their own professional corporations. Physicians collectively own the business and hire nurses, physician extenders, and clerical workers, who are the real wage workers in these settings.

Physicians are also capable of responding to changes in the industry and of modifying corporate forms they find most onerous. Thus, in response to the medical staff-HMOs that actually employ doctors, physicians and hospitals have developed "independent practice associations" (IPA-HMOs) and "preferred provider organizations" (PPOs) that maintain greater physician autonomy and the capacity to effect the size and shape of their own markets. Whereas only a minority of physicians are actually employed by HMOs, many others are affiliated with IPA-HMOs and PPOs while maintaining their individual and group practices. Furthermore, even when physicians have admitting privileges at for-profit hospitals, they do not work under proletarianized conditions but have incomes and working conditions similar to physicians with admitting privileges at nonprofit hospitals [32].

The future of physicians' power, occupational status, and class position is bound up with the trajectory of change in the larger political economy and in the health care industry. However, it is unlikely that doctors will fall into the working class because even if physicians were dominated and exploited by corporate managers, they would still participate in the domination and exploitation of subordinate workers. This view is consistent with recent developments in the class analysis of professional and managerial positions, in which Wright and others view professionals and managers as occupying "contradictory class positions" between capital and the working class [33]. Thus, increased employment in the most undesirable work settings will certainly result in lower income and greater bureaucratic control, which in turn may result in collective responses by the most disadvantaged members of the medical profession. However, employee physicians are likely to continue to dominate subordinate workers and to share in the surplus. The income of physicians is over five times greater than the income of RNs and seven to eight times that of LPNs and nurses' aides. Even institutionally employed physicians have incomes four times greater than RNs and six to seven times that of nonprofessional nursing workers [34].

Because changes in the industry are ongoing, any conclusion must be tentative. If the majority of physicians end up actually employed by capitalist corporations or managed care institutions in which they do not exercise any governing power and are unable to establish professionally controlled enclaves within these bureaucratic organizations, then the situation will have changed significantly; physicians will be subject to a major decline in power at the institutional level. However, during the period of this study, the decline of the medical profession appeared limited to a diminution of power within the health care system as a whole, and as the case of Pacific Hospital suggests, a limited loss of power within health care institutions.

Reorganizing the Tripartite at Pacific Hospital

Only a relative decline in physicians' power accompanied the ascendance of corporate management at Pacific Hospital. Both physicians and trustees participated in the governance of the hospital and the corporation, and in fact, the redistribution of power within the tripartite led to a greater coordination of interdependent roles and responsibilities, integrating dominant elites [35]. However, corporatization and elite realignment/integration did not occur without creating strain and even conflict within and among elite groups. Nevertheless, had physicians suffered an absolute decline in power, they might have aligned themselves with nurses and subordinate hospital workers. Despite conflict within the governing tripartite, this type of realignment did not occur.

Prior to corporate restructuring, the governing tripartite of Pacific Hospital consisted of the hospital administrator and a relatively small staff, the hospital's board of trustees, and the organized medical staff.

As Pacific Hospital reorganized, the hospital itself was reduced to the level of a subsidiary company. The hospital administrator, now referred to as the President of Pacific Hospital, reported to the President of Pacific Hospital Affiliates, who in turn reported to the President of Pacific Hospital Care Corporation, the parent holding company.

As administrators increased both in numbers and in power, the allocation of space devoted to the managerial function reflected this shift. Corporate executives (non-physicians recruited for their business expertise) and their staffs moved out of the hospital and occupied a separate office building in a business complex, where they were surrounded by other corporate offices and banks.

Although physicians and trustees were now more dependent upon the expertise of corporate executives, from the initial phase of corporatization, administrators had sought the cooperation of physicians and trustees in planning for the hospital's reorganization. All parties had been concerned about external pressures to contain provider costs as well as by increased market competition, and had participated together in the decision to undergo corporate restructuring and in the hiring of executives to reorganize the hospital into a regional health care corporation.

Even after corporate managers assumed overall command of holding company operations, the continued cooperation of the medical staff and the board of trustees was necessary for the long-term success of the reorganization plan. At Pacific Hospital, physicians were typical in that they were not employed by the hospital and independently maintained both individual and group practices. They generated revenues for the hospital by admitting patients and by ordering the use of the hospital's equipment and facilities. This gave the medical staff a great deal of leverage, and managers continued to seek physicians' involvement in the corporatization process. Furthermore, according to a physician informant, the medical staff would not have agreed to the reorganization without guarantees of continued participation in the governance of the hospital and corporation. As a result, representatives of the medical staff served on all boards, including that of the corporate holding company.

Corporatization also provided another form of elite integration, that of shared equity in new businesses. Physician groups continued to profit from internal businesses in departments such as pathology, radiology, and respiratory therapy, financial arrangements that had led Etzioni to discuss "the profit in nonprofit hospitals" even before the corporatization of community hospitals like Pacific [36]. Moreover, with expansion and diversification, managers and physicians developed new forms of shared equity on the periphery of Pacific Hospital. This included joint ventures in laboratories, home health care, magnetic resonance imaging centers, clinics, and Pacific's own HMO and PPO [37].

Nevertheless, the reorganization of the hospital did not occur without producing strain and conflict within the governing tripartite. Tension existed within the administrative hierarchy because the consolidation of corporate functions reorganized and threatened some positions in the prior administration. Corporate executives were accused of being insensitive to long-time administrative employees of the hospital who were worried about retaining their positions or losing their retirement. Some of these employees felt threatened by corporate staff members who were often younger, possessed more advanced degrees, and had broader business experience. A few members of the old staff, including department heads, were in fact promoted, but others reached a plateau in their careers, were demoted or eventually pursued careers in other organizations.

Corporatization and the ascendance of managers also created tension, and, at one point, a confrontation between corporate managers and physicians. As Pacific Hospital was reorganized into Pacific Health Care Corporation, some physicians became increasingly uncomfortable with the effect of corporatization on the organizational goals and culture of the hospital. Although physicians shared a business ethos through their participation in the governance of the hospital, equity in corporate businesses, and ownership of private practices, their occupational role diverged from that of managers in that physicians also had a professional and legal responsibility for patient care. Physicians were directly exposed to patients and to conditions on nursing wards during their daily visits to the hospital, while corporate managers rarely visited the wards and were oriented almost exclusively to expanding revenues and controlling hospital costs. Tension was high in the mid-1980s when a respected physician and chair of a medical committee brought these concerns to the attention of trustees in a letter than complained of a decline in employee morale and in the quality of patient care on the wards. The nursing staff was described as "pushed to the limit" under conditions of reduced support services. In assigning responsibility for changes that were considered detrimental to patient care, the letter charged that corporate executives had displaced the hospital's service orientation with a business orientation to the "bottom line" [38].

It was impossible to know the full extent of physician dis-satisfaction, but shortly afterward, trustees, corporate executives, and representatives of the medical staff went into a weekend retreat at a resort conference center. Workers were unable to observe the proceedings, but as a result of internal decisions within the govern-ing tripartite, the top executive of Pacific Hospital Affiliates, who appeared to be the primary target of physicians' discontent, was replaced. The chief executive officer of Pacific Corporation then resigned and was replaced by the former top administrator of Pacific Hospital, who had led the reorganization effort but moved on to assume an executive position at a major health care financial institution. A physician informant confided that physicians had played an instrumental role in dismissing the chief executive officer of Pacific Hospital Affiliates and that the choice of replacements reflected the desires of the medical staff and the board of trustees. Corporate managers controlled the daily operation of the corpora-tion, but executives had misjudged the countervailing power of other elites.

Although physicians played a decisive role in this conflict with corporate executives, their dissatisfaction with corporate arrange-ments should not be overemphasized. As I have shown, rather than proletarianize physicians, the ascendence of corporate management resulted in a relative decline in physicians' power, restructuring rela-tions among elite groups within the governing tripartite. While obvi-ously concerned about conditions on the wards and in support depart-ments that affected the care of their patients, physicians continued to align themselves with administrators and trustees rather than with subordinate workers.

Throughout this period of rapid institutional change, physicians continued to dominate the medical division of labor in the hospital. Their status above nurses and other hospital workers was clearly evident, even in informal interactions. When physicians visited their patients on the wards they sometimes spoke casually with one another about what amounted to luxury consumption, relating personal accounts of vacations and travel, expensive automobiles and residences while in the presence of subordinate workers whose social class back-ground and income were below their own. Yet, physicians avoided discussing corporate politics in front of these workers. If physicians were proletarianized to any significant degree, one would expect they would be inclined to readily share information about policies that were in fact having an adverse affect on hospital workers. This rarely occurred, and physicians never collectively aligned themselves with nurses or other hospital workers.

CORPORATIZATION AND SUBORDINATE WORKERS

We have seen that with changes in the political economy of the industry, hospitals that were financially capable of doing so reorganized into diversified and integrated health care corporations. I have maintained that although the balance of power shifted with the growth of corporate management, physicians and trustees continued to participate in the governance of these institutions. In the remainder of this chapter I argue that the more serious costs of corporatization fell not on physicians, but on subordinate production workers. At the same time that administrative overhead increased and hospitals invested in new businesses, corporate managers attempted to contain labor costs and increase productivity. Because labor costs remained the largest share of hospital operating expense, managers resisted unionization drives and took a harder stance in collective bargaining. Furthermore, they attempted to boost productivity by increasing the work load and cutting support services. The reorganization of nursing on hospital wards was at the center of these changes.

Containing Labor Costs:
Collective Bargaining in Harder Times

Until recently, hospital workers were denied the rights gained by workers in other industries. The earliest unions of hospital workers were organized in the 1930s, yet paternalistic relations between the majority of employers and employees extended well into the postwar period. The Taft-Hartley Act of 1947 excluded workers employed in private, nonprofit hospitals from coverage by federal labor laws. Nevertheless, with the continued growth of the industry in the post-World War II period, hospital workers engaged in a more widespread effort to unionize. The Service Employees International Union and Hospital Workers Union 1199 focused on organizing the growing number of nonprofessional workers who worked in auxiliary nursing, housekeeping, laundry, and food service departments of hospitals. The majority were women and disproportionately women of color who held the least desirable hospital jobs. Inspired by the Civil Rights Movement, these workers were receptive to collective action and their unionization held the promise of revitalizing the labor movement. Between 1961 and

1973, nonprofit hospitals with collective bargaining contracts increased from 4 to 14 percent and further gains seemed likely as federal legislation was pending that would protect hospital workers' right to unionize [39].

Threatened by the prospect of unions organizing RNs, the leadership of the American Nurses' Association (ANA) was forced to include collective bargaining within its professional activities, particularly in geographical areas where unions were strong: the major urban areas of the Northeast, the Great Lakes Region, and the West Coast. Beginning in the late 1960s, the ANA rescinded its "no-strike" pledge, supported legislation to protect the right of hospital workers to engage in collective bargaining, and began to use the strike as a means of advancing RNs' occupational interests. Many RNs were influenced by the women's movement and sought to redress issues of gender inequality. Their willingness to engage in struggles to improve RNs' wages and working conditions was brought to the nation's attention by the San Francisco nurses' strike of 1974. In June, just two months before the passage of the 1974 amendment to the Taft-Hartley Act that legitimized union organizing and collective bargaining in the industry, 4,400 RNs represented by the California Nurses' Association walked out of San Francisco Bay area hospitals. The strike received national attention as thousands of RNs from all over the country were attending the ANA's convention in San Francisco at the time [40].

Despite greater rank and file activism and the adoption of more militant tactics, the ANA's strategy remained distinct from that of hospital unions representing nonprofessional workers. As a professional association, the ANA was engaged in efforts to advance the occupational interests of RNs. Although similar in this way to a craft union, the ANA distanced RNs from the labor movement and from nonprofessional hospital workers by its emphasis on professionalization and occupational mobility.

After 1974, the unionization of hospital workers was expected to spread rapidly as workers were now protected by federal labor laws. In fact, the proportion of nonprofit hospitals with collective bargaining contracts did increase from 14 percent in 1973 to 20 percent in 1976 [41]. However, the larger economy was now in decline, and hospitals were under increasing pressure to contain costs. Although hospital labor costs were actually a declining proportion of total operating expenses, they remained the largest single item of expense, and containing these costs could offset growing administrative overhead while contributing to the availability of capital for new investments. So, despite the fact that hospital workers had only recently attained rights other workers had gained in the 1930s and 1940s, health care managers adopted strategies then being used in other industries to contain wages and benefits. Where unions were attempting to organize, managers resisted, hiring consultants to help conduct sophisticated anti-union campaigns. Where workers were already organized, managers took the offensive in collective bargaining, legitimizing their demands for concessions by using the cost containment environment to their advantage [42].

In their efforts to resist unions and contain labor costs, hospital administrators soon found that the new legislation institutionalizing collective bargaining could work to their benefit. As with the bureaucratization of labor relations in other industries, managers were able to use the requirements of the National Labor Relations Board (including bargaining unit decisions, notification of contract expirations, strike notices, required mediation, and so on) to weaken unionization drives and unions' capacity to engage in effective strikes [43].

In taking the offensive against hospital unions, managers typically targeted nonprofessional workers in food service, housekeeping, laundry, and auxiliary nursing—workers who provided the basis of union strength. Although RNs' positions were more secure, managers took a tougher stance with them as well. Thus, in June and July of 1984, ten years after the 1974 San Francisco nurses' strike, 6,300 RNs in Minneapolis-St. Paul were forced to engage in the largest RN strike to date to keep hospital managers from reducing full-time positions and increasing involuntary part-time employment [44].

Collective Bargaining at Pacific Hospital during Corporatization

As Pacific Hospital underwent corporate restructuring and diversified into new businesses, management also engaged in efforts to contain labor costs. Unlike many hospitals, Pacific's workers were already organized for collective bargaining. Nonprofessional workers, including auxiliary nurses, ward clerks, and workers in dietary, housekeeping, and laundry were represented by a local of the Service Employees International Union (SEIU). RNs were represented by the California Nurses' Association (CNA) which had initiated the 1974 RN strike at San Francisco Bay area hospitals.

Throughout the 1970s and 1980s, management took an aggressive posture in contract negotiations. A strike by nonprofessional workers represented by SEIU began shortly after my employment in 1979 as a part-time ward clerk. As I walked the picket line, I learned from other workers that the corporation was attempting to roll back gains in wages and benefits attained in prior years.

I also learned that although SEIU and the CNA were progressive organizations, they had a history of limited corporation. An underlying antagonism seemed to exist between nonprofessional service workers and RNs. The SEIU local had not supported the RNs' strike in 1974, and nonprofessional service workers, including auxiliary nurses, had weakened the strike by continuing to work as RNs walked the picket line. In turn, during the 1979 SEIU strike, nonprofessional workers were bitter because the CNA did not fully support their strike and because RNs continued to work on the wards.

During the next several years in which I worked at the hospital, contracts with both the SEIU and the CNA expired in 1983 and 1985, each time a couple of months apart, but neither the union nor the professional association pursued mutually expiring contracts. Management began each period of negotiations by announcing a budget cut and demanding concessions in wages and benefits. Placed on the defensive, RNs and nonprofessional workers mobilized separately to resist corporate demands.

Threatened by pending changes in reimbursement by Medicare, not long before contract negotiations began in 1983 Pacific announced a plan to cut operating expenses by 6 percent, claiming that cutbacks were necessary because of declining revenues. Before contracts expired, employees received letters warning of "wholesale layoffs" and "cuts in spending." Although few workers were actually laid off, management continued a gradual reduction in auxiliary nurse staffing that had begun in the mid-1970s through attrition and shifting workers to other work sites outside the hospital. In addition, laundry, dietary, housekeeping and central supply reported reductions in full-time positions and hours. In contrast, RN staffing had increased substantially during the 1970s and early 1980s and was not directly affected.

Throughout the negotiations, both the SEIU and CNA focused on fighting corporate demands for concessions and were relieved when the corporation rescinded most of its demands during final contract negotiations. Although avoiding concessions was a significant achievement given the adverse collective bargaining environment of the 1980s, SEIU and CNA failed to challenge the shift in auxiliary nurses' employment and reductions in nonprofessional support services that had been implemented without negotiation or organized resistance. A similar pattern was repeated two years later.

Prior to contract negotiations in 1985, Pacific announced another budget cut, this time of 10 percent. Managers transferred many of the remaining nurses' aides to employment in a convalescent hospital the corporation had recently acquired. In addition, sixty full-time equivalent positions in nonprofessional support services were to be eliminated or have their hours reduced. Budget cuts and further demands for concessions on wages and benefits again created anxiety, and workers were relieved when the CNA and SEIU settled negotiations separately in June and July of 1985 without major concessions. As in 1983, RN staffing was unaffected, but both organizations failed to resist changes that displaced ancillary workers and adversely affected working conditions on the wards.

Throughout this period, Pacific Corporation continued to diversify rapidly into new businesses and expand corporate administrative staff. Under external pressures to contain health care costs, management appeared to be shifting part of the cost of corporate restructuring onto production workers, using the national health care expenditure crisis as a rationale for budget cuts, and the greater confidentiality of the holding company to facilitate their efforts. Thus, although management held meetings with employees ostensibly to explain the need for cost-cutting measures, a corporate financial disclosure was never made. Meanwhile, workers throughout the hospital were more harried.

Increasing Productivity

While the displacement of auxiliary nurses and the reduction of ancillary support staff were largely overshadowed by corporate demands for concessions on wages and benefits, these changes were part of Pacific's corporate effort to increase productivity. Similar developments were occurring throughout the industry. Furthermore, as Karen Sacks has shown, managerial strategies to increase productivity differed depending upon the position of workers in the occupational hierarchy [45]. Nonprofessional service workers in support departments were likely to be treated differently from semiprofessional and paraprofessional workers. Understanding how management pursued different means to accomplish the same end provides an important context for understanding the reorganization of nursing work.

Nonprofessional hospital workers include a variety of occupations that support the production of nursing care on hospital wards. Many of these occupations were established as nursing developed historically, shedding housekeeping, laundry, food service, and clerical tasks onto workers lower in the occupational hierarchy. Nonprofessional hospital workers are typically uncredentialed or credentialed through vocational programs. They are also likely to have working class backgrounds, and minorities are overrepresented among them [46]. At Pacific Hospital, virtually all service workers were members of SEIU, and as a ward clerk I often interacted with them when they came to the ward to clean rooms, move patients, deliver food trays or laundry. The jobs they performed were more similar to work in fast food, janitorial, or domestic services than to occupations higher in the hospital hierarchy and more closely linked with the dominant profession of medicine. For example, work in the food service department was organized much like an industrial assembly line, with a detailed division of labor and rationalized work processes broken down into subdivided tasks.

Nonprofessional workers at Pacific Hospital, like the service workers studied by Sacks at Duke Medical Center, were vulnerable to staff reductions and subject to work intensification and closer supervision [47]. Corporate management increased the work load of these workers at the same time that they imposed tighter systems of labor control. For example, housekeeping workers had greater autonomy than workers in food service or the laundry because they moved throughout the hospital cleaning patients' rooms. However, like many other hospitals, Pacific elected to subcontract the management of these services, in this case to the Service Master Corporation, whose supervisors increased the surveillance of housekeeping workers while implementing a speedup. Other departments used scientific management principles to further subdivide work and implement closer supervision of more clearly differentiated tasks.

Higher up the occupational hierarchy, allied health care professions perform technical tasks that have differentiated with the medical division of labor. These diverse occupations include therapists, technologists, and technicians in departments such as physical therapy, respiratory therapy, laboratories, and radiology. Their work is critical to medical production, but their tasks are more narrowly defined than that of nursing, which is often considered a semiprofession at the top of this paraprofessional hierarchy [48].

Unlike nonprofessional workers, the reorganization of work among paraprofessional and semiprofessional workers at Pacific Hospital was accompanied by the upgrading of credentialing requirements and the downgrading of less credentialed members of the occupation. These changes were also characteristic of larger trends in the industry. As Sacks found at Duke Medical Center, technicians and therapists trained on the job or through hospital-based certification programs were likely to be replaced by graduates of more advanced educational programs, a process that worked against disadvantaged working class and minority workers [49].

Although the upgrading of credentialing requirements was typically associated with professionalization and a higher occupational status, in actuality, work was often intensified. As less credentialed workers were downgraded or displaced, upgraded workers were frequently assigned a larger range of tasks, including some of the more routine work previously performed by less credentialed workers. As a ward clerk and later a "monitor tech," I experienced the process myself [50]. Moreover, I interacted with a variety of workers, including respiratory therapists, phlebotomists, and lab technicians who took pride in upgraded credentials at the same time that they complained about the greater demands upon them. However, because I did not work in their departments, it was difficult for me to distinguish genuinely upgraded tasks and responsibilities from the addition of routine tasks that simply increased the volume of work. Because of the diversity of paraprofessional occupations, the situation within each occupation was probably somewhat different [51]. Nonetheless, credential upgrading corresponded with a marginal level of professionalization and a greater work load. A similar reorganization of work was occurring at the top of the paraprofessional hierarchy, at the very center of hospital production, and because of my position on nursing wards, I was able to observe the change first hand.

Reorganizing Nursing

Throughout most of the post-World War II period, many nonprofessional nurses worked in hospitals under the supervision of RNs. In fact, LPNs and nurses' aides comprised the majority of hospital nursing personnel and performed the bulk of routine bedside care. However, beginning in the 1970s, hospital administrators began replacing LPNs and aides with RNs, so that by the mid-1980s RNs constituted the majority of hospital nursing personnel [52].

The displacement of auxiliaries and the reorganization of the division of labor on hospital wards occurred as the political economy of the health care industry shifted to cost containment. Throughout the

1970s and 1980s, the postwar expansion of *hospital* employment for less credentialed nurses slowed at the same time that their employment on the periphery of hospitals grew. As hospitals reorganized into diversified health care corporations, the displacement of auxiliaries facilitated the staffing of new peripheral work sites. LPNs and nurses' aides were often shifted to employment in outpatient clinics, nursing homes and home health care. Industry wide, work in peripheral sites does not pay as well as hospital jobs. Home health aides, for example, earn about half the wages earned by nurses' aides in hospital employment, and their hours are typically less stable [53].

Phasing auxiliary nurses out of hospital employment was a sensitive issue. As we have seen, hospital service workers had only recently begun to attain the rights, wages, and benefits achieved by workers in other industries. Given the class and racial stratification of American society and the overrepresentation of working class and minority women in auxiliary nurse positions, this policy institutionally discriminated against the more disadvantaged workers. Yet, for several reasons, health care managers were able to avoid public debates over the issue. First, the reorganization of nursing was made incrementally throughout the 1970s and 1980s as individual hospitals gradually increased their employment of RNs. Also, the majority of auxiliaries were displaced through attrition and shifts to other work sites rather than through the mass layoffs and unemployment that accompanied the displacement of industrial workers in core manufacturing industries during the 1970s and 1980s. Finally, the displacement of auxiliaries appeared to be the unfortunate corollary to professional upgrading, which in turn seemed inevitable with advances in medical knowledge and technology.

Although union activists at Pacific Hospital suggested to me that management may have implemented the change in order to weaken hospital unions, I argue that the principal managerial motivation was increasing productivity. Certainly the displacement of nonprofessional nurses from hospital wards occurred during a critical phase in the unionization of hospital workers. In addition, hospitals are also central work sites in the industry, and LPNs and nurses' aides are important to union strength. Displacing auxiliary nurses had an adverse affect on hospital unionization as LPNs and nurses' aides were typically moved to smaller, scattered work sites. Nevertheless, while the detrimental effect on unions may have been a contributing factor in managerial decisions, it cannot explain the reorganization of nursing labor. The majority of hospital workers were unorganized, and only a minority were ever involved in unionization drives [54]. Yet the displacement of auxiliaries and the reorganization of nursing work occurred at hospitals nationwide. Under the pressures of cost containment, administrators throughout the industry shared an interest in increasing the productivity of hospital workers.

Furthermore, as I pointed out in the Introduction to this study, the reorganization of nursing served interests other than those of management. In fact, the reorganization of nurses' work actually began with *occupational* rather than managerial initiatives. In the late 1960s and early 1970s, a segment of nursing educators and administrators became increasingly dissatisfied with nursing's failure to achieve full professional status. They claimed that "team nursing" with RNs and auxiliaries performing differentiated tasks had deprofessionalized the occupation. In contrast, "primary nursing" with RNs performing "total patient care" was supposedly based on professional principles that had existed in private duty nursing before RNs were ever employed in hospitals and before the creation of a stratified work force. In returning to professional principles of practice, tasks would be reunified and RNs would have a one-to-one relationship with their patients.

When I began this study I believed that the trend toward primary nursing and an all-RN staff could be easily explained by advances in medical knowledge and the professionalization of nursing. However, observations on nursing wards and study of prior forms of nursing labor convinced me that this explanation was inadequate.

In Part Two I examine different forms of nursing labor in order to understand the recent reorganization of the division of labor on hospital wards during the cost containment era. To assess the claim that team nursing deprofessionalized nursing and that primary nursing reprofessionalizes the occupation by returning to principles embodied in private duty nursing, it is necessary to begin with the organization of nursing practice before RNs were employed in hospitals. Chapter 3 discusses hospital apprenticeship and private duty before the post-World War II period, when hospital wards were staffed by nurse apprentices and the majority of RNs (then known as "graduate nurses") worked outside hospitals. Chapter 4 follows with an analysis of the organization of team nursing in the 1950s and 1960s when a stratified work force was employed by hospitals to perform differentiated tasks. In Chapter 5, I examine the development of primary nursing in the 1970s and 1980s and the trend toward an all-RN work force performing reunified tasks. This includes a detailed case study of the organization of work at Pacific Hospital.

NOTES

1. Paul Starr, *The Social Transformation of American Medicine* (New York: Basic Books, 1982), 430. For additional information on for-profit hospitals, see Donald W. Light, "Corporate Medicine for Profit," *Scientific American* 255(6) (Dec. 1986): 38-45; Bradford H. Gray, *For-Profit Enterprise in Health Care* (Washington: National Academy Press, 1986).

2. Debates about issues of ownership and control were discussed in a variety of reports and publications, including Arthur Anderson and Co. and the American College of Hospital Administrators, *Health Care in the 1990s: Trends and Strategies* (privately published, 1984); Regina E. Herzlinger and William S. Krasker, "Who Profits from Non-Profits?," *Harvard Business Review* (Jan.-Feb. 1987): 93-106; J. Rogers Hollingsworth and Ellen Jane Hollingsworth, *Controversy about American Hospitals*: Funding, Ownership, and Performance (Washington: American Enterprise Institute for Public Policy Research, 1987); J. Warren Salmon, "Profit and Health Care: Trends in Corporatization and Proprietization," *International Journal of Health Services* 15(3) (1985): 395-418; Starr, *Social Transformation of American Medicine,* book 2, chap. 5.

3. See Rosemary Stevens, *In Sickness and in Wealth* (New Haven: Basic Books, 1989); Eli Ginzberg, *The Medical Triangle* (Cambridge, Mass.: Harvard University Press, 1990), chap. 2.

4. Paul J. DiMaggio and Walter W. Powell, "The Iron Cage Revisited: Institutional Isomorphism and Collective Rationality in Organizational Fields," *American Sociological Review* 48(2) (1983): 147-160.

5. For general discussions of corporatization, see Starr, *Social Transformation of American Medicine,* 428-444 and Stevens, *In Sickness and in Wealth,* chap. 12. Corporate integration and diversification are discussed in detail in Jeff Goldsmith, *Can Hospitals Survive?: The New Competitive Health Care Market* (Homewood, Ill.: Dow Jones-Irwin, 1981); Montague Brown and Barbara McCool, *Multiple Systems Strategies for Organization and Management* (Rockville, Md.: Aspen, 1980); Montague Brown, "Systems Diversify with Ventures Outside the Hospital," *Hospitals* (1 Apr. 1981): 147-153.

6. For an excellent discussion of the financial and legal advantages of the health care holding company, see Frederick H. Kerr, "Considering a New Structure: The Health Services Holding Company," *Law, Medicine and Health Care* (Oct. 1983): 214-219.

7. R. Neal Gilbert, "Corporate Restructuring Works for California Hospital," *Hospital Financial Management Journal* (Sept. 1982): 16.

8. Dennis J. Patterson and Kent A. Thompson, "Product Line Management: Organization Makes the Difference," *Healthcare Financial Management* (Feb. 1987): 66-72; Ralph G. Goodrich and G. Richard Hastings, "St. Luke's Hospital Reaps Benefits by Using Product Line Management," *Modern Healthcare* (15 Feb. 1985): 157-158.

9. Eileen Appelbaum and Cherlyn Skromme Granrose, "Hospital Employment under Revised Medicare Payment Schedules," *Monthly Labor Review* (Aug. 1986): 40.

10. Anne Kahl and Donald E. Clark, "Employment in Health Services: Long-Term Trends and Projections," *Monthly Labor Review* (Aug. 1986): 27. Apparently many hospitals were able to successfully implement such strategies. In 1987 the Congressional Budget Office reported that hospitals had profited under PPS reimbursement since the program was implemented. Profit levels were reported between 12 and 15 percent in 1984, 17.6 percent in 1985, and 15.7 percent in 1986. *New York Times,* 29 Mar. 1987, p. 1.

11. For example, an industry survey reported that 52 percent of surveyed hospitals had increased their surpluses in 1984, the first year that the PPS/DRG system was in effect. Fifty-eight percent of these profitable institutions increased their surplus between 1 and 20 percent, 33 percent increased their surplus between 21 and 100 percent, and 9 percent acknowledged doubling their profits. "NRC Survey," *Modern Healthcare* (16 Aug. 1985): 87.

12. Starr, *Social Transformation of American Medicine,* 437.

13. Before the post-World War II expansion of the health care industry, women were more likely to be represented among hospital administrators. The precise statistics vary. Barbara Melosh, *The Physician's Hand* (Philadelphia: Temple University Press, 1982) indicates that nurses administered at 28 percent of general hospitals in 1925 (p. 163). Susan M. Reverby, in *Ordered to Care* (Cambridge: Cambridge University Press, 1987), conveys that nurses were superintendents at 41 percent of all hospitals in 1933 but were concentrated in small and church- affiliated institutions (p. 107). Males were more likely to hold positions at large institutions and with the professionalization of hospital administrators and the differentiation of nursing administration, males dominated the governance of postwar hospitals.

14. Unless otherwise indicated, the discussion of Pacific Hospital and its reorganization is based on field notes, interviews with informants, hospital and corporate literature, and newspaper accounts as well as several industry publications that I have not identified to maintain the institution's anonymity.

15. *New York Times,* 25 Jan. 1987, p. 1.

16. Charles Perrow, "Goals and Power Structures: A Historical Case Study," in *The Hospital in Modern Society,* ed. Eliot Freidson (New York: Free Press, 1963), 112-146.

17. For the growth of administrative personnel and overhead, see David U. Himmelstein and Steffie Woolhandler, "Cost Without Benefit: Administrative Waste in U.S. Health Care," *The New England Journal of Medicine* (13 Feb. 1986): 441-445. The authors point out that administrative costs in

Canada under a national health insurance program, and in Britain under the National Health Service are much lower.

18. Linda I. Collins, "Executive Salaries to Rise 6.1 Percent in '86," *Hospitals* (16 Oct. 1985): 104-120.

19. Perrow, "Goals and Power Structures," 113.

20. Stevens, *In Sickness and in Wealth*, 340.

21. Eliot Freidson, *Professional Dominance* (New York: Atherton, 1970); also Eliot Freidson, *Profession of Medicine* (New York: Dodd, Mead and Co., 1970; Chicago: University of Chicago Press, 1988).

22. Starr, *Social Transformation of American Medicine,* book 2, chap. 5; The Changing Character of the Medical Profession, [special issue] *Milbank Quarterly* 66(supplement 2) (1988).

23. Vicente Navarro, "Professional Dominance or Proletarianization?: Neither," *Milbank Quarterly* 66(supplement 2) (1988): 57-75.

24. George Ritzer and David Walczak, "Rationalization and the Deprofessionalization of Physicians," *Social Forces* 67(1) (1988): 1-22.

25. John B. McKinlay, "Toward the Proletarianization of Physicians," in *Professionals as Workers*, ed. Charles Derber (Boston: G. K. Hall, 1982), 37-62; John B. McKinlay and Joan Arches, "Towards the Proletarianization of Physicians," *International Journal of Health Services* 15(2) (1985): 161-195; John B. McKinlay and John D. Stoeckle, "Corporatization and the Social Transformation of Doctoring," *International Journal of Health Services* 18(2) (1988): 191-205.

26. See Charles Derber, "Toward a New Theory of Professionals as Workers: Advanced Capitalism and Postindustrial Labor," in *Professionals as Workers,* ed. Charles Derber, 193-208. Interestingly, Derber has since shifted his view and argued that medicine and the professions generally constitute a new class. See Charles Derber, William A. Schwartz, and Yale Magrass, *Power in the Highest Degree: Professionals and the Rise of a New Mandarin Order* (New York: Oxford University Press, 1990). For criticisms of the thesis that the professions are becoming proletarianized, see Eliot Freidson, *Professional Powers* (Chicago: University of Chicago Press, 1986), chap. 6. And, for a recent critique of Freidson by a writer sympathetic to the proletarianization thesis, see David Coburn, "Freidson Then and Now: An 'Internalist' Critique of Freidson's Past and Present Views of the Medical Profession," *International Journal of Health Services* 22(3) (1992): 497-512.

27. See Magali Sarfatti Larson, *The Rise of Professionalism* (Berkeley: University of California Press, 1977), chap. 11.

28. Eliot Freidson, "Occupational Autonomy and Labor Market Shelters," in *Varieties of Work,* ed. Phillis L. Stewart and Muriel G. Cantor (Beverly Hills: Sage, 1982), 39-60; also *Professional Powers.* Even a semiprofession such as nursing may improve its status through employment in formal organizations and bureaucracies. In chap. 4, I discuss how nurses'

autonomy and expertise have actually increased with their withdrawal from the private duty market and employment in hospitals. However, nurses also remained subordinate to physicians and hospital administrators.

29. Doctors in private practice had an average net income of $118,600 in 1985, 5 percent above the average for all physicians. However, institutionally employed physicians earned an average of $80,400 for the same year, 29 percent below the average for the profession. American Medical Association, *Socioeconomic Characteristics of Medical Practice, 1986* (Chicago: Center for Health Policy Research, 1986), table 2.

30. For further data regarding these characteristics, see American Medical Association, *Socioeconomic Characteristics of Medical Practice, 1984* (Chicago: Center for Health Policy Research, 1984); *Socioeconomic Characteristics of Medical Practice, 1986*; Survey and Data Resources, *Physician Characteristics and Distribution in the U.S., 1984* (Chicago: American Medical Association, 1984); *American Medical News,* 13 Feb. 1987, p. 17.

31. In 1985, 25.7 percent of non-resident patient care physicians were actually employed: 9.7 percent by hospitals, 2.7 percent by government, and 13.3 percent in other settings, including HMOs. American Medical Association, *Socioeconomic Characteristics of Medical Practice, 1986*, 2.

32. For information on variation among HMOs, see California Hospital Association, *Hospital Fact Book, 1985* (Sacramento: California Hospital Association, 1985), table 2.15; *American Medical News,* 2 Jan. 1987, pp. 10-11; 16 Jan. 1987, p. 7. On physicians with admitting privileges at for-profit institutions, see American Medical Association, "The Role of Profit in Medicine," SMS Report (Nov. 1983).

33. For discussions, see Erik Olin Wright, *Classes* (London: Verso, 1985); Erik Olin Wright, "What is Middle About the Middle Class?," in *Analytical Marxism*, ed. John Roemer (Cambridge: Cambridge University Press, 1986), 114-140; Martin Oppenheimer, *White Collar Politics* (New York: Monthly Review Press, 1985).

34. *Facts About Nursing, 84-85* (Kansas City: American Nurses' Association, 1985), table 4.26; *Facts About Nursing, 86-87* (Kansas City: American Nurses' Association, 1987), table 5.4. For physicians' income, see source in n. 29.

35. For a similar view of the reorganization of power within health care organizations, see W. Richard Scott, "Managing Professional Work: Three Models of Control for Health Organizations," *Health Services Research* 17(3) (Fall 1982): 213-239.

36. Amitai Etzioni and Pamela Doty, "Profit in Not-for-Profit Corporations: The Example of Health Care," *Political Science Quarterly* 91(3) (Fall 1976): 433-453.

37. Such arrangements were not unique to Pacific but characteristic of developments in the industry. See Robert Rosenfield, "Market Forces Set

off Skyrocketing Interest in Hospital-Doctor Ventures," *Modern Healthcare* (1 May 1984): 70-74; Lawrence Gerber, "A Sampling of Joint Venture Opportunities for Hospitals and Physicians," *Trustee* (May 1985): 38-43; *Wall Street Journal*, 23 Jan. 1987, p. 23.

38. Unless otherwise indicated, this section is based on case study material in author's possession.

39. C. Schoen, "The Labor Movement in Health Care: USA," in *Industrial Relations and Health Services,* ed. Amarjit Singh Sethi and Stuart J. Dimmock (New York: St. Martin's Press, 1982), table 4.2. For additional discussion of hospital unionization, see David Denton, *The Union Movement in American Hospitals: 1847-1976* (Ph.D. diss., Boston University, 1976).

40. For a critical analysis of this strike, see David Gaynor et al., "RN's Strike: Between the Lines," in *Prognosis Negative: Crisis in the Health Care System,* ed. David Kotelchuck (New York: Vintage, 1976), 229-245. For a larger discussion of the ANA's activities in strikes and collective bargaining, see Rita E. Numerof and Michael N. Abrams, "Collective Bargaining Among Nurses: Current Issues and Future Prospects," *Health Care Management Review* 9(2) (Spring 1984): 61-67; U.S. Dept. of Labor, *Impact of the 1974 Health Care Amendments to the NLRA on Collective Bargaining in the Health Care Industry* (Washington, 1979), 88-97.

41. Schoen, "Labor Movement in Health Care," table 4.2. In 1976 the total for all hospitals was 23.1 percent. The sector breakdown was as follows: federal—80.7 percent, state and local—22.4 percent, non-profit—19.7 percent, profit—10.8 percent.

42. *Service Employee* (the monthly newspaper of the Service Employees International Union), Feb.-Mar. 1986, pp. 5-7. For discussions of labor relations during this period, see Leon Fink and Brian Greenberg, *Upheaval in the Quiet Zone* (Urbana: University of Illinois Press, 1989); Karen Brodkin Sacks, *Caring by the Hour* (Urbana: University of Illinois Press, 1988).

43. Fink and Greenberg, *Upheaval in the Quiet Zone,* 167-168.

44. For an analysis of the strike, see Philip A. Kalisch and Beatrice J. Kalisch, "Nurses on Strike: Labor-Management Conflict in U.S. Hospitals and the Role of the Press," in *Political Issues in Nursing,* ed. Rosemary White (New York: John Wiley and Sons, 1985), 105-151.

45. Sacks, *Caring by the Hour.*

46. Ibid.; Fink and Greenberg, *Upheaval in the Quiet Zone.*

47. Sack's study complements my own. Whereas I focus primarily on changes in nursing wards, Sacks focuses on nonprofessional hospital workers in support departments during the cost containment era of the 1970s and 1980s. Her work includes excellent descriptions, not only of a unionization drive, but of work in housekeeping and food service departments. See *Caring by the Hour,* chap. 7.

48. For a discussion of the occupational division of labor in health care, see Freidson, *Profession of Medicine,* chap. 3.
49. Sacks, *Caring by the Hour,* chap. 8.
50. Initially a ward clerk, I later became a "monitor technician." With minimal training, I moved from working as a nonprofessional clerical worker to what sounded like a paraprofessional technical worker. "Monitor techs" received three days of training in a hospital-based certification program and a small wage differential that failed to offset the additional tasks and stress involved in an expanded work load that included watching cardiac monitors while retaining all the routine duties of ward clerks. Monitor techs were also shifted to a nonunion job classification, as if to reinforce their supposedly more "professional" status.
51. In some cases, paraprofessional workers actually feared downgrading. For example, respiratory therapists were concerned that management would shift their tasks back to RNs.
52. I discuss the details of this transition in chap. 5.
53. Appelbaum and Granrose, "Hospital Employment under Revised Medicare Payment Schedules," 45.
54. See Denton, *Union Movement in American Hospitals.*

PART TWO

Reorganizing
Nursing Labor

CHAPTER 3

Before the Postwar Period: Hospital Apprenticeship and Private Duty

Before the Great Depression nursing care in hospitals was produced by nurse apprentices or untrained attendants. Nurse apprentices resided in hospital training schools and worked as unpaid labor in an authoritarian system that put a higher priority on the extraction of labor than on the quality of nurses' training. After several years of labor on hospital wards, graduates left with a marginal education to enter private duty nursing in patients' homes, where they were now free of the authoritarianism of the hospital and training school and somewhat independent of physicians as well. As contemporary nursing leaders have pointed out, private duty nurses had an individual, direct relationship with patients and were responsible for the patient's complete nursing care. Nevertheless, as I will explain, neither apprenticeship training nor private duty nursing established a professional form of nursing practice. Although free of institutional domination, rather than attain occupational autonomy and control over their work, graduate nurses experienced market coercion and new forms of domination. Unable to monopolize the private duty market or control access to employment, they suffered intense competition from untrained nurses. In addition, once employed by private households, they were subject to the power of patients and their families and had great difficulty maintaining a work jurisdiction exclusive of domestic labor. Some tried to find work in other settings, particularly as private duty "specials." However, as the private duty market failed during the 1930s, hospitals began to employ graduate nurses, eventually displacing the apprenticeship system. During the 1940s, nurses' aides and practical nurses were widely introduced as well, creating a stratified work force in postwar hospitals.

HOSPITAL APPRENTICESHIP:
EXPLOITATION AND INSTITUTIONAL DOMINATION

Throughout the nineteenth century, an occupational role for trained nurses had yet to be clearly established. Hospitals existed primarily for the poor and recruited former patients and untrained attendants to work on the wards. Until the 1920s, most people were nursed in their own households, sometimes by a practical nurse, typically an older woman who had acquired experience through the care of friends and neighbors as well as her own family members. Although their work was only marginally differentiated from women's domestic labor, practical nurses dominated the paid nursing work force before schools were established to produce graduate nurses [1].

The first training schools for nurses were begun in the 1870s, but the majority were founded between 1900 and 1920, at the same time that many hospitals were established. While only 430 schools existed at the turn of the century, by 1920 there were almost 1,800, most of them affiliated with hospitals [2]. The earlier training schools were founded by an elite of upper and middle class women who hoped to create a professional occupation for women like themselves. However, the aspirations of nursing leaders were soon thwarted by hospitals' role in the development of training schools.

Exploitation and the Organization of Work

The early training schools were patterned after the British Nightingale system. However, whereas Nightingale advocated that nursing schools be financially independent of hospital authorities and under the separate authority of professional leaders and administrators, in the United States most schools were established by hospital authorities and physicians. As a result they were financially dependent and organizationally subordinate to the larger institution [3].

The dependence of nursing schools on hospitals not only compromised the ability of nursing superintendents to govern schools but jeopardized the professional training of graduate nurses. Except for elite institutions founded by nursing leaders, the majority of schools were established to provide a cheap and disciplined work force to replace untrained attendants. Since nursing care was the major service hospitals produced, establishing a nursing school was an investment in the production and supply of the hospital's principal workers. Thus, in investigating training programs in the 1920s, Burgess concluded that "the student nurse is worth money! Nursing is probably the only profession where students are eagerly sought because of their economic value" [4].

Although nursing superintendents attempted to maintain the standards of their schools, institutional needs for ward labor clearly prevailed over occupational goals of professional training. For the most part, apprentices were workers rather than students, and their labor was virtually unpaid. In discussing the political economy of hospital apprenticeship, Ashley indicates that

> nurses were expected to pay for their own education by subjecting themselves to up to three years of labor in institutions that gave few returns equal to the value of that labor . . . a system that was more exploitative than educational [5].

Apprentices toiled for long hours on hospital wards and received a meager room and board and a minimum of formal instruction in return. Burgess reported a workweek of up to sixty-five hours in the 1920s with an average of fifty-five, far above that of blue-collar industrial workers [6]. Apprentices were often required to work seven days a week with a half day off on Sundays, and while an eight to nine hour day was the norm in the better schools, some hospitals still worked apprentices twelve hours a day. Work loads were heavy and in some cases apprentices worked split shifts. Formal instruction was commonly given in the afternoon or evening after a hard day of work. In addition, superintendents sometimes hired apprentices out to private households to care for patients in their homes. The apprentice remained unpaid, but hospitals generated additional revenues through this practice [7].

Upon admission, new apprentices were introduced into an institutional work process on hospital wards. There were several methods of organizing work, each foreshadowing later approaches to the organization of nursing wage labor in hospitals. In the better schools, work was organized by combining "graded training" with what became formally known as the "case method." In graded training, nursing superintendents assigned work according to apprentices' experience. Advanced apprentices were assigned the more acutely ill patients while junior apprentices were assigned convalescent patients. When graded training was combined with the case method, the apprentice was responsible for performing each patient's complete care. Because the case method provided the opportunity to learn the entire range of nursing tasks, it was usually considered the best method for training purposes [8].

In most schools however, training was compromised by the demand for labor. Apprentices were assigned a number of patients, and with a heavy work load, it was difficult to perform complete nursing care for each patient. Consequently, the case method was often modified by a task approach, which first developed informally as apprentices and head nurses faced the demands of a multiple patient assignment. Several apprentices could be assigned specific tasks that needed to be done for all patients, lightening the work load for other nurses. This included both specialized and routine tasks. Thus in graded training, senior apprentices were often assigned not only the most acutely ill patients but also tasks that required greater skill or responsibility, such as administering medications or charting. In turn, junior apprentices were not only assigned convalescent patients, but routine low-level tasks (e.g., housekeeping) which they could easily do and which relieved advanced apprentices of this work [9].

In the worst institutions, "ungraded training" failed to distinguish among students until they reached the last year of training. Here, apprentices were not only exploited, they were more likely to experience their work as drudgery. Thus, Goldmark found nurses who had been in training from a few months to two years performing identical work. When ungraded training was combined with a task approach, the work was even more difficult. Junior apprentices were often assigned exclusively to routine tasks rather than the complete care of patients. In such institutions, both first and second year students were found giving baths, making beds, and along with new apprentices, performing a heavy burden of non-nursing work. The boredom and fatigue of being confined to low-level tasks and dirty work until the advanced stages of apprenticeship were likely to contribute to exhaustion and students' withdrawal from training programs [10].

Although not particularly efficient when combined with ungraded training, the task approach became formally known as the "functional method" and was associated with scientific management and the search for the most efficient method of performing work. As Reverby has argued, nursing leaders were interested in scientific management as early as the progressive period before World War I [11]. In addition, the disciples of Frederick Taylor seemed eager to apply their science to hospitals and nursing. Frank Gilbreth, an associate of Taylor, had been interested in hospitals since the early decades of the century and pioneered "motion study," in part, by filming surgical procedures in hospitals. At a national nursing convention in 1912 Gilbreth proposed rationalizing hospital organization, and at a convention of the American Hospital Association two years later, he continued to be "highly critical of the hospitals' lack of standardization and haphazard organization of work" [12].

Nevertheless, although scientific management was of growing interest to segments of the nursing profession, apprentices' unpaid labor and an extended workday inhibited the systematic application of these principles to the organization of nursing work on hospital wards. Hospital superintendents believed they were already staffing with the cheapest labor available. Until nursing wage labor replaced the apprenticeship system, management lacked incentive to rationalize the labor process [13].

Furthermore, not only were hospital superintendents uninterested in rigorously applying Taylor's methods of work simplification, nursing leaders and superintendents were likely to be ambivalent. Some apparently believed that scientific management principles might be useful in upgrading nurses' training by separating nursing from non-nursing tasks and hiring subsidiary workers to perform housekeeping, laundry, and kitchen work. However, nursing superintendents had little interest in applying such principles to nursing care itself, which was based on traditional methods rather than the analysis and determination of the most efficient approach. "Tasks were learned through constant repetition and adherence to each hospital's 'one right way,' not the 'one best way,' of performance" [14]. In addition, nurses' skills were grounded in gender and the development of character and a commitment to duty rather than on technical skills or theoretical knowledge that could be rationalized and systematized [15]. And, although the benefits of scientific management might extend beyond economic efficiency to enhance superintendents' control over nurses, the apprenticeship system of institutional domination was not threatened or in need of replacement.

Producing Trained Nurses: Stratification and Institutional Domination

The authoritarian hierarchy of the hospital and the training school can be compared with social relations in the patriarchal family.

Physicians and hospital superintendents, the patriarchs of the institutional household, dominated apprenticed nurses, who were expected to defer to their authority and to demonstrate appropriate social behavior, such as standing when they entered the wards. Although apprentices were considered the handmaidens of physicians with responsibility for carrying out their medical orders, apprentices also labored under the immediate authority of a female nursing hierarchy in the training school. This hierarchy was headed by the nursing superintendent or matron, a graduate nurse drawn from the elite who attended the better nursing schools. Ward supervisors or head nurses were either graduate nurses hired for supervisory work or advanced apprentices. Below them were apprentice-workers, the dependents of the hospital household [16].

Although authoritarianism may be traced to hospitals' religious and military heritage, social relations in American hospitals and training schools in the early decades of this century can be more directly attributed to hospital superintendents' desire to maintain the apprenticeship system of labor. Authoritarianism served the larger institutional interests of hospital authorities in extracting the unpaid labor of apprentices. Thus, Lavinia Dock,

> one of the early leaders of American nursing, stated succinctly:
> "Discipline and strict subordination of the school makes it possible
> for the hospital to exact from [the nursing students] an amount of
> work it would be quite impossible to exact from women over which
> it had no special hold" [17].

Nevertheless, the authoritarian culture that prevailed in the institution was not imposed simply by hospital superintendents and physicians. Training schools themselves were based on the need for order and strict discipline, which served to meet not only the demands of hospital work but the separate process of producing graduate nurses. As Reverby has argued, this was a feature of the Nightingale system that training schools in the United States did retain. Like Nightingale, nursing superintendents believed that discipline was necessary to develop the appropriate qualities of the professional nurse. Nurses in training were "apprenticed to duty." Through the rigor of the training school experience, their virtues as women capable of self-sacrifice and commitment could be further developed to create a respectable occupation superior to that of untrained nurses [18].

The ideal candidate for this transformative process embodied qualities not only rooted in gender but in social background, a woman whose socialization in an upper or middle class family had provided the "character" that could be brought to fruition through the discipline of the training school. It was from this interlinking of gender and social class that the occupational image of the professional nurse providing selfless care to the victims of war and disease was derived [19].

In order to accomplish their mission of transforming women into professional nurses, nursing schools hoped to attract young women with the appropriate class background to begin with. In part, they succeeded. Trained nurses have always been a more privileged occupational group when compared to the occupations of most women. This was even more so before the 1930s when women who worked for wages commonly labored as domestic servants [20]. Nursing leaders desperately wanted to separate their occupation from association with women who performed such work. Nevertheless, as recent social histories have emphasized, with the development of the occupation, trained nurses became internally stratified by social class. Since the early decades of this century, the class background and experience of apprentices in most training schools differed from that of nursing's elite, whose more privileged class backgrounds enabled them to pursue careers as educators, public health nurses, or nursing superintendents after training in the more elite schools. With the rapid growth of hospitals and training schools, the efforts of nursing leaders to professionalize the occupation were hindered by the changing class composition of nursing recruits. To meet the need for nurses to staff hospital wards, superintendents were forced to draw upon women from lower middle class and working class backgrounds. As Melosh relates, "superintendents could not always hold out for well-bred ladies. . . . As the nursing work force grew, the genteel women of the first schools necessarily gave way to a less rarefied breed" [21]. Consequently, according to Reverby, "nursing leaders complained during the 1920s that women with the 'right character' and 'proper home training' were not applying to nursing school. . . . By the late 1910s and 1920s, . . . nursing was attracting more working-class than middle-class women to its ranks" [22].

Despite the changing social class composition of nurses in training, the ideal nurse was still described in the 1920s as a woman of "good breeding" [23]. Nursing leaders and those supporting their professional objectives were often disdainful of women whose class background was less than middle class. Burgess argued that "these undereducated, unprepared women make trouble within the profession. Many of them are drawn from a social group which is not strictly professional in character" [24]. Although her remarks were disparaging, Burgess was candid about the reason hospital and nursing superintendents recruited lower class women. "It seems to be a fact that hospitals can utilize . . . young women of rather low grade. The hospital is always tempted to admit such women in order to get the great volume of its work done" [25].

Nursing leaders were worried by the growing class stratification within nursing. Burgess feared that working class women might proletarianize nursing in that they were

> the ones who are talking trade unionism for nurses. It is natural that they should. Their fathers, brothers, and sweethearts are ardent members of trade unions. . . . Somehow these undereducated women, of inadequate social and academic background must be kept out of the profession [26].

As Reverby points out, Burgess' "fears about unionism were based mainly on future possibilities" rather than an immediate threat [26]. The real fear for nursing leaders was that women from less affluent class backgrounds were likely to compromise, if not defeat, elite efforts to create a middle class profession.

Burgess even claimed that nursing recruits from the lower classes altered the institutional purpose of the training school, turning it into a reform school for women of inferior grade [27]. It is no doubt true that apprentices from working class and lower middle class backgrounds compromised the Nightingale ideal and made the transformative process of producing women with appropriate "character" more difficult. While this probably affected the organization and culture of the training school, as we have seen, strict discipline and authority were considered necessary even to the development of nurses with appropriate class backgrounds.

The authoritarian culture of the training school began upon admission when apprentices "were required to sign an agreement expressing, in the words of one, 'their willingness to obey all rules, to be subordinate to authorities . . . and to conduct themselves as members of a noble profession' " [28]. Once enrolled, nursing superintendents and head nurses directly supervised the labor of apprentices and continually reinforced the rules and procedures that apprentices were required to follow.

Nursing schools combined labor, the reproduction of labor, and training within the same institution. They were total institutions in that authoritarianism prevailed in all three spheres of activity [29].

Apprentices were required to reside within the institution and were subject to as much regimentation in their off-duty hours as in their hours on the wards. Rules existed for virtually every activity, from when apprentices rose in the morning to when they slept at night. Mealtimes were strictly regulated and superintendents routinely conducted inspections of living quarters. Apprentices were socially isolated from their families and the larger community, and paternalistic rules existed regarding leaving the premises, curfews, and visitors. According to Burgess,

> the tradition of the hospital training schools is such that every student who enters is subjected to almost continuous supervision, in . . . almost incredibly minute detail. For three years practically every act of the student's waking life is known, checked, and controlled [30].

Regimentation could extend to the most intimate aspects of apprentices' lives. Melosh points out that "in an extreme example, . . . [an] article urged superintendents to record each student's menstrual periods, to provide 'anti-constipation' diets, and to segregate 'fat and lean' groups in the dining room, with appropriate foods for each" [31].

The authoritarianism of hospitals and training schools remained in the minds of their graduates for years. In the 1950s, Burling interviewed nurses whose thoughts probably captured the sentiments of many others looking back on their experience: "Never once in the whole time did I express an opinion on anything. None of us did, we just did exactly what we were told and never asked questions." Another communicated that the experience of institutional domination was more taxing that the actual work and long hours on the wards. "You felt exhausted all the time and it was the tension more than the work" [32].

Nevertheless, the institution never completely dominated apprentices. Even in authoritarian systems, there are always informal means of "making out" [33]. In the daily life of the training school, individual and group efforts to influence the behavior of head nurses and superintendents were common. The head nurse was often a senior apprentice herself and experienced conflicting allegiances as she served in a supervisory role while being dependent upon fellow apprentices to get the work done. Apprentices often formed cliques to cooperatively facilitate their progression through the training program and to lessen the burden of work and institutional authority. In addition, as Melosh has shown, apprentices' work culture not only socialized nurses into occupational norms, traditions, and techniques but also into the informal norms of institutional life [34].

Apprentices endured the severity and exploitation of training schools for several reasons. In deciding to become nurses, they were strongly influenced by their gender socialization. Despite the drudgery of apprenticeship, nursing provided a socially acceptable occupational role, one linked with women's traditional gender role and requiring less of a break from that experience. In addition, apprentices were typically young, single women who often had been encouraged by their families to attend nursing schools [35]. Parents could safely send their daughters to training schools with the assurance that they would be under the paternal authority of male doctors and hospital superintendents and the immediate authority of nursing matrons.

As suggested earlier, nursing also provided opportunities for both middle class and working class women to participate in the paid labor force at a level higher than that of most working women. In the first three decades of this century women's occupational choices were quite limited. Only 24 percent of women worked in the paid labor force in 1920 [36]. For middle class women, nursing was one of the few occupations other than teaching that was close to their own class background and professional aspirations, as well as to social norms regarding women's work. These women had no interest in working as domestic labor, and unlike clerical occupations, trained nurses provided a sense of professional calling and duty. For working class women, nursing furnished a means of occupational, if not class mobility. These women did not have as much choice in whether to work for wages, and nursing schools provided them an opportunity to acquire training for an elite women's occupation with the major resource they did possess—their capacity to labor.

Furthermore, although training schools were compromised by hospital requirements for ward labor, they still served occupational as well as institutional purposes. Young women entered apprenticeship programs because they wanted to become trained nurses. Nursing schools, despite their deficiencies, controlled access to graduate status. If apprentices ever hoped of attaining that status, they had to submit to an authoritarian system of occupational socialization and institutional control. Thus, ultimately, apprentices' participation was voluntary. For those who endured, the Nightingale ideal ideologically supported the need for discipline while other apprentices provided social support and camaraderie. When apprentices had doubts about their chosen occupation, as many surely did, they reminded themselves that, although long and difficult, apprenticeship was temporary, a transition to a full occupational status. While acknowledging that "the discipline of a nursing school is severe," Burgess noted that "students accept the strict discipline for three years because they know that it is in the nature of an initiation which will finally open the door to freedom" [37]. For the majority of graduates the door to "freedom" was private duty nursing.

PRIVATE DUTY:
INDEPENDENCE AND NEW FORMS OF DOMINATION

Before the 1930s, hospitals were uninterested in employing their own training school graduates, to whom them would have to pay wages and whose continued cooperation was uncertain. Hospital superintendents preferred students who would work as unpaid labor and submit to the authoritarian culture that existed on the wards. Even nursing superintendents held ideological beliefs that justified the apprenticeship system and devalued their own graduates. According to Burgess, many superintendents "seem to feel that students are keener, more alive, more loyal; that they lose something precious as soon as they enter the nursing profession as graduates" [38]. What graduate nurses actually lost was their willingness to cooperate with the exploitation and authoritarianism of the apprenticeship system. The overwhelming majority entered private duty nursing, where they hoped to find work appropriate to their new occupational status.

On entering private duty nursing, apprentices were free of institutional domination. They no longer had to submit to the drudgery of long hours on hospital wards or to the authority of hospital and nursing superintendents and the regimentation of the training school. Graduate nurses were at liberty to make their living as trained nurses. And, once they accepted employment, rather than a multiple patient assignment on hospital wards, they now had a one-to-one relationship with individual patients and could employ the case method to its full potential, performing each patient's complete care [39].

Nevertheless, although private duty had definite advantages over hospital apprenticeship, the occupational status of the graduate nurse was ambiguous at best. Private duty can be interpreted variously as professional practice, the practice of a craft, and as domestic household employment. Present-day nursing leaders have looked back upon private duty as a professional form of practice. Frustrated with the organization of nursing in hospitals, they identify the one-to-one relationship between nurse and patient and the unity of tasks in providing patients' complete care as the essence of professional practice [40].

Some recent historical interpretations support this view. Although Wagner is critical of nursing leaders and their desire to professionalize the occupation, in an effort to sustain an argument that nurses have become proletarianized through their employment in hospitals, he argues that private duty nurses were autonomous professionals with control over their work [41]. Nursing historian Barbara Melosh also stresses the independence of private duty nurses by calling them "freelancers." However, Melosh argues that private duty was a form of craft labor that enabled nurses with less privileged social class backgrounds to resist the professionalization of the occupation and to exercise skills learned in apprenticeship programs. While acknowledging the shortcomings of private duty, Melosh's interpretation of the historical development of nursing parallels that of contemporary nursing leaders in that she identifies recent trends toward reunifying tasks as a return to an earlier craft tradition. Melosh has simply replaced the ideal of *professional* autonomy and control with that of *craft* autonomy and control [42].

It can also be argued that private duty nursing was a form of domestic labor. Private duty nurses were employed by patients and their households, and typically worked in the residences of their employers by the hour, by the day, or for longer assignments. Frequently they were on duty twenty-four hours a day until the patient recovered or the household terminated their employment, which as we shall see, often included housework. The private duty market had been dominated for decades by practical nurses who performed similar work and were never thought of as independent professionals, but were considered hired workers barely superior to domestic servants. Although nursing leaders hoped to create a separate occupational status and profession, only the rather marginal distinction of having a hospital diploma degree separated graduate nurses from untrained nurses, and ultimately from female domestic labor at the bottom of the services hierarchy [43].

Was private duty nursing a form of independent professional practice, a craft, or household domestic labor? Actually, private duty was an ambiguous form of labor that is not adequately defined by any one of these occupational labels. Training schools had demanded a great deal of unpaid labor and provided only a marginal education. Although private duty nurses were free of apprenticeship exploitation, they were certainly not self-employed professionals, and as I will explain, neither did they control their work. It can be argued that apprenticeship training created a craft culture and practice, but as I indicated earlier, the skills of trained nurses were actually based as much on gender and class background as on technical skills. In addition, the idea of craft control over nurses' work was as problematic as that of professional control. A strong craft or profession establishes closure by controlling its labor market and access to employment. Graduate nurses were unable to do so in private duty nursing and as a result experienced intense competition with practical and untrained nurses. Furthermore, once employed, graduate nurses were subject to new forms of domination that further inhibited their autonomy and control.

An Open Labor Market

As graduate nurses left training schools, they entered a labor market that was becoming increasingly oversupplied with workers. With the rapid establishment of training schools during the first two decades of the century, the number of graduate nurses increased from approximately 12,000 in 1900 to over 200,000 by 1930. During the 1920s, the number of graduate nurses surpassed that of practical nurses, and by 1934 the Committee on the Grading of Nursing Schools reported that "during the past 30 years the population of the United States has increased 62%, while the number of trained nurses has increased 237%" [44].

At the same time that the private duty market became saturated with nurses seeking work, the demand for services was limited and soon declined. Before the 1920s, private duty nurses were more likely to be employed by both middle class and wealthy families. As the economy faltered, it became more difficult for middle class families to afford the services of private duty nurses. And, when they did hire such workers, they were more likely to consider employing practical nurses who were willing to engage in housework as well as nursing [45].

Not only was demand for private duty services limited, graduate nurses were unable to monopolize the market or create effective shelters to protect them from competition with untrained nurses. Graduate nurses claimed to offer upgraded services and hoped to establish an occupational jurisdiction above practical and untrained nurses, but they had difficulty doing so. Hospital diploma credentialing did not provide an adequate basis for monopolizing the private duty market, and although some graduates used the title of "registered nurse" or RN, registration and licensing were not yet mandatory and formal credentialing was often unnecessary for many nursing assignments. Furthermore, other means of sheltering professional occupations from market competition were also wanting. Unlike physicians, graduate nurses did not establish independent practices or professional corporations. And, as I will discuss later, their employment by private households was a poor institutional base for controlling their work [46].

In the absence of a professional or craft monopoly, graduate nurses were vulnerable to competition from untrained workers who were able to substitute in performing work now claimed by graduate nurses as properly belonging to them. Although practical nurses were not formally trained, they had acquired a pragmatic knowledge of nursing practice, and untrained nurses with experience in hospitals without training schools had also acquired some knowledge of nursing procedures. Even women with less experience but who had done housework, nursed family members, or perhaps worked in domestic service were able to compete in the private duty market. Having previously dominated the market, practical nurses and untrained women used a variety of tactics to find needed employment and became rather adept at claiming to be credentialed themselves. When asked, some acknowledged they were not graduate nurses, but stated that they were registered. Others claimed to be graduates, although their diplomas were from correspondence schools [47].

With the influx of graduate nurses into the private duty market, correspondence courses and a variety of short courses proliferated for uncredentialed nurses determined to continue making a living in private duty. The organizers of the courses justified their programs by arguing that there was a need for subsidiary nurses below the graduate nurse level. Although not particularly kind in his portrayal of these workers, William James Mayo, founder of the Mayo Clinic, defended the production of "sub-nurses" in 1920, maintaining that "the public needed 'other types of nurses less highly trained but nevertheless important social service vehicles, the Fords, so to speak of the nursing world'". Others were entirely unsympathetic to graduate nurses and to efforts to professionalize the occupation. For example, John Dill Robertson, founder of the Chicago School for Home and Public Health Nursing, stated that his short course prepared nurses who

> for the great bulk of nursing . . . are quite as capable as the graduate nurse. Often they are more desirable because they are willing to do housekeeping as well as nursing, and in its final

analysis, nursing is nothing more nor less than housekeeping for the sick [48].

The pressures of market competition frustrated graduate nurses and created hostility toward practical nurses. Having sacrificed themselves for three years in apprenticeship programs, graduate nurses were resentful and accused untrained nurses of being incompetent domestic servants who had somehow managed to attain the rewards and status of graduate nurses. As one nurse complained:

> Why should nurses go in training for three years and endure the hardships, when maids are hired on the same salary as a graduate nurse? Absolutely never have given a bath, made a bed, or taken temperatures, cannot comprehend, do not know what the word responsibility means, and personally feel they are on a par with the graduate nurse [49].

Since untrained nurses had often given baths, made beds, and taken temperatures, we may be skeptical of the objectivity of such opinions, but they clearly reveal the adversity of the open market and the effects of competition.

To make matters worse, graduate nurses were unable to control access to private duty employment. The majority of private duty nurses were referred by physicians and registries, of which there were several different types. Commercial registries were often associated with untrained nurses and domestic workers; hence most graduate nurses found employment either through hospital registries, which prevailed over independent nursing registries, or through direct referral by physicians [50].

Hospital registries did help to shelter graduate nurses from competition with untrained nurses, but these agencies primarily served the interests of hospitals and were not under graduate nurses' control. Hospitals refused to concede the private duty market to their own graduates, occasionally referring practical nurses as well, and as mentioned earlier, "hiring out" apprentices in order to realize additional revenues. Furthermore, hospital registries generated competition among graduate nurses themselves, who were dependent upon these agencies for employment. Forced to compete for referrals, nurses often complained that registries were unfair. Many felt that particularistic criteria, including favoritism, age, and personal contacts influenced whether one received steady or desirable employment. Since registries controlled access to needed jobs, they were also able to pressure nurses to take undesirable assignments, as failure to maintain good relations with registries could inhibit steady employment, and blacklisting could keep one from working at all [51].

After hospital registries, the most common means of attaining employment was through direct referral by physicians. As with registries physicians' control over access to private duty practice resulted in nurses' dependency and contributed to competition among nursing workers. Physicians often referred practical nurses as well as graduate nurses, primarily because households requested them for their greater willingness to perform housework. To ensure regular referrals, graduate nurses had to remain on good terms with physicians as well as meet their expectations on the job. On the whole, physicians preferred graduate nurses, who were more likely to have social backgrounds similar to their own and whom they believed to be more disciplined in the care of patients [52].

Nevertheless, with the private duty market oversupplied with labor and demand contracting, the continued participation of untrained nurses in the market often thwarted graduate nurses' efforts to find adequate employment. By the late 1920s, the typical graduate nurse was unemployed for a total of five months out of the year and had to struggle to find regular assignments [53]. As market conditions deteriorated, nursing leaders became increasingly concerned about the underemployment of graduate nurses and the inability of the profession to control competition from untrained workers. Some segments of the leadership thought that practical nurses should simply be prevented from working as nurses. Others recognized they were unlikely to keep nonprofessional nurses out of the occupation and believed it was more realistic for graduate nurses to gain control over these workers. The Goldmark Report of 1923 had proposed that professional nursing create and support the training and credentialing of subsidiary nurses under professional nursing's control. However, by 1928 market conditions had deteriorated further, and Burgess was hostile to the idea of subsidiary nurses, suggesting that these "servant girls" were no longer needed [54].

As nursing leaders debated strategies, graduate nurses were increasingly disillusioned with the "freedom" to which they had aspired as nurse apprentices. Without market shelters under nursing's control, intense competition and dependency prevailed over occupational autonomy. The organization of private duty practice would further compromise graduate nurses' control over their work.

Household Domination and Nurses' Dissatisfaction

Graduate nurses were not only constrained by an open labor market and registries' and physicians' control over access to employment, but once employed, nurses had difficulty establishing a professional work jurisdiction as they were subordinate to physicians, and more importantly, to the patient and their household.

Free of institutional domination, private duty nurses were no longer under the direct authority of nursing supervisors and performed nursing care independently of physicians' direct observation. Private duty nurses cared for the patient over the course of their illness, while the doctor visited only occasionally to check on the patient's condition and to make changes in medical orders. Nevertheless, the nurse remained subordinate to the doctor, who exercised control indirectly. Although the physician did not pay the nurse's wages, the need for the nurse's presence was determined by the physician in consultation with the patient and household. Only the physician had the authority to diagnose the patient, determine the medical treatment, prescribe orders, and determine whether nursing care was medically necessary. Physicians appreciated nurses who could give adequate care, make the patient comfortable, follow medical orders, and accurately observe and report changes in the patient's condition. For the most part the physician did not directly observe the private duty nurse's work performance, but the doctor did assess the overall success of the nurse in completing her assignment and had the ultimate power in deciding whether to continue referring the nurse to patients, registries, or other physicians [55].

Moreover, the potential autonomy of the private duty nurse was severely limited by the dominance of patients and their households. When formal organizations mediate relations between professional and client, the professional has some protection from the power of the client to define the work to be done. In contrast, in private duty nursing, the patient and their household were the employer as well as the client and consumer of the nurse's services. Rather than professionalize nursing, the unmediated relationship between the nurse and the patient provided a basis for the patient and household members to define and control the nurse's work. Thus, according to Kalisch and Kalisch, "the nurse's time was considered the property of anyone who employed her," enabling households to largely dictate the conditions of employment and exercise power over the work to be performed when they so desired [56]. If a nurse objected, the patient or household members could complain to the physician that the nurse was uncooperative, or use the ultimate sanction—dismissal of their employee. The nurse then reentered the fierce competition of the private duty market.

The power of patients and their households also jeopardized the graduate nurse's ability to maintain a clear distinction between her role as a trained nurse and the work of practical nurses and domestic workers. Patients and household members could demand that the graduate nurse perform tasks outside her desired work jurisdiction, and the nurse was in a weak bargaining position. Not only did the patient and their household control her wages, the graduate nurse's work jurisdiction was not clearly defined. The nurse's unmediated relationship with the patient and responsibility for the patient's complete nursing care made the boundaries of that care amorphous and unclear. In addition, graduate nurses were unable to keep practical nurses from using the title of "nurse" and from engaging in domestic work as well as nursing. Because housework was threatening to graduate nurses' desired occupational status, they no doubt did a great deal of hidden work in attempting to negotiate the limits of their work jurisdiction. In the process, some learned to avoid situations and types of patients that were likely to require work they considered undesirable. However, by doing so, they also reduced their own employment opportunities by creating niches for practical nurses who would readily do twenty-four hour shifts, housework, or take postpartum and other patients associated with a higher level of domestic work tasks [57].

Private duty nurses were typically employed by middle and upper class households. The working class and the poor were cared for by family members or in hospitals, and were visited by public health nurses. Still, the distinction between middle class and upper class households could affect the graduate nurse's work experience significantly. This was because the presence or absence of servants made an important difference in the kinds of problems the nurse encountered. In lower-middle class homes servants were unlikely to be present, and consequently the nurse might well be asked to perform a broad range of tasks, including housework. In contrast, the upper-middle class and the wealthy often employed servants. If such households were not simply hiring a graduate nurse to solve their servant problems, the private duty nurse was less likely to be called upon to perform domestic work [58].

In wealthy households, the problems of the graduate nurse resulted from the class disparity that usually existed between the nurse and household members, and from the graduate nurse's efforts to maintain an occupational status superior to that of the servants. Often of lower middle or working class background, the private duty nurse typically felt insecure or oppressed in upper class households. Family members were not solicitous of her efforts to establish herself as a member of a respected profession, and they often found it difficult to tolerate her class inferiority. Thus, the graduate nurse

> not infrequently . . . spoke bitterly of how she was "treated like a servant," because the family, perhaps, did not ask her to join them at meals or did not give her the guestroom. . . . Without considering that her nursing education had not included one course in the humanities, they found her conversation uninteresting or her reading tastes deplorable. She, in turn, was likely to consider such families snobbish, cold, exigent in their demands, and unappreciative of her services [59].

At the same time, the graduate nurse's efforts to maintain an occupational status above the servants often made the situation more difficult. Domestic servants, aware of the nurse's marginality, were often offended by her claim to a superior station.

As we have seen, graduate nurses were caught between the demands of less affluent households for domestic work that professional nursing was attempting to disassociate itself from, and the snubs of upper class households whose members recognized the graduate nurse's inferior class background and weak claim to professional status. Unable to comfortably accept doing domestic housework in less affluent households, at the same time the graduate nurse was averse to nursing for the upper classes, a "species of patient most threatening to the private nurse's self-respect" [60].

Dissatisfied with household employment, graduate nurses who could pursue employment in other branches of nursing often did so. Some were able to move on to public health nursing. Centered initially in the settlement houses of Chicago and New York, public health nursing included a variety of public agencies and visiting nurses' associations that served the poor. Graduate nurses' employment in public health nursing grew from 4 percent in 1912 to a peak of approximately 20 percent in the mid-1920s, before declining to 8 percent of employed nurses by 1950 [61]. However, during the 1920s particularly, public health nursing provided an important means of escaping the problems of private duty, at least for some segments of the occupation. This branch of nursing was attractive in that graduate nurses were no longer employed by households and were able to clearly separate themselves both from domestic work as well as from the undesirable aspects of serving upper class households. Melosh indicates that some graduate nurses "left their wealthy patients with open relief," one indicating that there was "greater satisfaction in doing for these poor unfortunates than in catering to patients who have lived lives of pampered luxury." Another stated, "You meet a class of people who need your care and advice. . . . One is more appreciated" [62]. At the same time, public health nurses remained independent of hospital and nursing superintendents and were more independent of physicians as well. Unfortunately, the majority of graduate nurses had little hope of entering public health nursing, which was always associated with an elite segment of the occupation composed of graduates from the better training schools. The elite often experienced a period of employment in private duty, but this was typically a temporary status to careers in public health, education, or supervisory work in hospitals.

Another alternative to private duty nursing was hospital employment, but it was a limited option as well. Under pressure to improve their programs, hospital training schools did hire graduate nurses for supervisory and instructor positions, but these positions were few in number and usually reserved for elite graduates. Because hospitals continued to staff their wards with nurse apprentices, jobs as staff nurses were scarce. Moreover, a graduate nurse who entered hospital employment in a non-supervisory position violated occupational norms.

> To do general duty in an ordinary hospital, . . . as a regular and not a temporary worker, at once implies that there is something the matter with the nurse. Nurses who have tried it report that except in a few hospitals they have been made to feel their inferiority keenly. Floor maids and orderlies, student nurses and interns, head nurses, supervisors, members of the medical and surgical staffs, and all other people connected with the hospital, seem to feel that for a nurse to do general floor duty after graduation indicates that she must have failed in the more dignified branches [63].

For the majority of graduate nurses, the most viable means of escaping the problems of work in private residences actually developed within private duty nursing. As health care services shifted from the home to the hospital, nurses began working as private duty "specials." These nurses were still employed by private households, but they took care of their patients in the hospital rather than at home. Private duty specials were ordered when the physician believed the patient's condition warranted the undivided care of a nurse or when a wealthy patient or their family wanted a private nurse. With the growth of hospital-based services in the 1920s, hospital registries were increasingly filling calls for specials, and by the end of the decade, the private duty market was largely divided between special work and home care [64].

Graduate nurses took advantage of work as specials to avoid the worst aspects of private duty employment. Despite the fact that specials were still employed by patients and their families, by limiting their care to hospitalized patients, nurses were no longer pressured to do housework, no longer had to deal with upper class family members on household terrain, and no longer had to manage difficult relations with domestic servants. Off the patient's home turf, they could limit the demands of patients while more clearly establishing a work juris-diction they felt appropriate to their occupational role. Thus, Melosh argues that

> while the nurse at home had to claim a precarious niche for herself in the routines and social relationships of the household, the hos-pital special worked in an environment tailored to medical and nursing routines. . . . The private patient in the hospital still retained the final prerogative of an employer, and could dismiss an unsatisfactory nurse. But short of this last recourse, the hospital patient lost much of his or her former power to define the content and practice of the nurse's work [65].

Furthermore, this organizational niche was acceptable to graduate nurses because they were able to avoid the authoritarian relations that still prevailed on hospital wards. Private duty specials worked in the hospital, but because they were employed by the patient, they were "independent of the rules, discipline and supervision of the hospital and its nursing hierarchy" [66].

Despite its advantages, working as a special was not a panacea. Graduate nurses were still unable to completely exclude practical nurses, a significant minority of whom also found employment as specials. Moreover, graduate nurses were also in competition with one another for this type of work, and most had to continue to work in home care at least some of the time to obtain needed employment. In addi-tion, access to employment remained under the control of hospital registries and physicians. The most serious problem, however, was that graduate nurses still lacked a stable work jurisdiction and occupational role. As Reverby states, "a special worked *in* the hospital, but she was not *of* the hospital." The work of the trained nurse "was still erratic and uncertain, her status continually ambiguous" [67].

The ambiguity of the private duty special's role created tension on the wards. According to Melosh "their work routines and relatively unsupervised practice threatened the discipline and hierarchy of the hospital" [68]. Since superintendents could not officially supervise the work of private duty specials, they took steps to ensure that specials remained separate from apprentices and did not undermine ward discipline and the ability of hospitals to continue to benefit from apprentices' unpaid labor. Excluded from social relations with other nursing workers, specials typically felt isolated at the patient's bedside. In turn, apprentices were burdened with a heavy work load and "resented the private-duty nurse's independence and more leisured pace" [69]. Consequently, despite the development of this hospital-based niche in the private duty market, Burgess still reported a high level of dissatisfaction among graduate nurses. For the majority, there was no escape from the problems of private duty nursing. Before alternatives that might have reorganized private duty under graduate nurses' control were adequately explored, the demand for these services contracted sharply with the onset of the Great Depression [70]. During the 1930s and early 1940s the majority of graduate nurses entered hospital employment as ward duty nurses, and with the inclusion of practical nurses and nurses' aides, a stratified labor force was created within hospitals.

NURSES ENTER HOSPITAL EMPLOYMENT: 1930 TO THE POSTWAR PERIOD

In the 1930s many middle class families were no longer able to employ private duty nurses whose services were now truly a luxury that only the wealthy could afford. Even when the economy began growing again after 1935, the private duty market could no longer provide adequate employment for the number of nurses seeking work. Surveys indicated that the majority of private duty patients continued to come from the upper strata of the population, and that the majority of Americans rarely used such services [71].

Meanwhile, during the depression, nurses suffered severe unemployment, worse than that of most occupations and exceeding the level of national unemployment. Nursing leader and historian Mary Roberts indicated that in some cases nurses were absolutely destitute, and that "it was necessary to equip many of them with shoes and uniforms before they could go on duty" [72]. At the height of the depression, nurses sought work in other industries, including the emerging airline industry, which employed some nurses as stewardesses but could not provide enough jobs to meet the flood of applications. Thousands of nurses also experienced intermittent employment. In 1933 and 1934, 10,000 found temporary jobs with the Civil Works Administration, but when the program was discontinued, the majority were again thrown back onto the labor market where they faced the likelihood of further unemployment [73].

Even before the crash, nursing leaders were considering the possibility that hospitals might provide a solution to graduate nurses' underemployment. In 1928 Burgess anticipated the obstacles involved as well when she commented that

> in institutional work there would appear to be a definite shortage, but is it one which can be looked upon as the solution for disposing of the horde of new workers? Apparently, almost all hospitals are seriously understaffed. Many of them have no graduate nurses at all for the care of their patients. Here, one would say, is the great untilled field for nursing. Perhaps it may be. If the nursing profession can persuade hospital authorities that the trained nurse is better for the care of patients than either the student or the attendant" [74].

During the worst years of the depression, nursing leaders were forced to respond to the unemployment crisis. They did so by initiating an effort to persuade hospital authorities to employ professional nurses for duty on hospital wards. In 1932, a committee of the American Nurses' Association (ANA) contacted hospitals throughout the country and encouraged the hiring of graduate nurses as paid employees to replace student apprentices. In their letter to hospital authorities, nursing leaders indicated that graduate nurses "were available and willing to work at low salaries" [75]. In addition, according to Reverby

> study after study began to appear in both the nursing and hospital management literature comparing student and graduate labor. The studies were attempts to convince hospitals and reluctant nursing superintendents that graduate nurses were more efficient workers, cheaper because of low wage demands, and easier to discipline both because of their professionalism and because they would be the hospitals' not the patients' employees" [76].

Nursing leaders suggested that apprentices' labor was not as cheap as supposed because of supervisory costs and the increased expenses that could be anticipated with endeavors to improve training schools.

The efforts of nursing leaders may have contributed to the transition that would take place, but they were certainly not decisive. Most hospitals ignored the pleas of nursing leaders and did not even bother to respond to their letter. In addition, there was no evidence that graduate nurses would be easier to manage than apprentices. Superintendents were well aware of graduate nurses' dislike of the hospital system. And, though nursing leaders attempted to convince hospital authorities of the economic advantage of staffing with graduates, Reverby indicates that nursing studies "were very idiosyncratic and ideologically motivated" [77]. It was not clear that a paid labor force would actually be cheaper than the apprenticeship system, and the shift to wage labor was likely to be irreversible without any guarantee that wages would remain low.

Nevertheless, as the industry began to reexpand in the mid-1930s, hospitals began hiring graduate nurses to staff the wards. Hospital authorities no doubt believed it in their interest to do so, as the future of the apprenticeship system appeared uncertain. With the publication of critical reports on the status of nursing by Goldmark and Burgess in the 1920s and 1930s, hospitals were under pressure to upgrade training programs. With reforms likely, the ability of hospitals to continue to extract unpaid labor by working apprentices long hours on hospital wards would be curtailed. If apprentices were replaced with a paid work force of trained nurses, hospitals would no longer be criticized for flagrantly exploiting nursing students, an important consideration with the continuing shift of services to the hospital and the centrality of nursing in hospital production. Furthermore, as Reverby has suggested, a critical factor may have been the development of insurance programs that enabled hospitals to overcome their financial vulnerability and to pass wage costs on to consumers through insurance premiums [78].

Once the transition began, it proceeded rapidly. As late as 1927, the ANA reported that over 70 percent of hospitals with nursing schools did not employ any graduate nurses for ward duty, but continued to staff with apprentices [79]. In addition, prior to the depression, hospitals without nursing schools continued to rely upon untrained attendants. During the 1930s, both types of institutions began to employ graduate nurses for ward duty. By the end of the decade, the majority of hospitals with training schools did so, and by 1941, "it was estimated that over 100,000 [graduate] nurses were employed as hospital staff nurses in institutions with or without schools" [80].

As nursing historians have shown, the transition from private duty to hospital employment was a difficult change for nurses. Although they needed employment, graduate nurses were reluctant to accept work in hospitals, which they associated with a return to institutional "drudgery, exploitation, and low status." Yet, for many, "dignity became a luxury." During the depression, nurses sought jobs not only on hospital wards but as housekeepers, laundry workers, or in other departments of the hospital, hoping to at least receive room and board [81].

On entering hospitals as staff nurses, graduates were forced back into an authoritarian system still organized around the exploitation and domination of apprentices. The work load was heavy, consisting of a multiple patient assignment to which graduate nurses were no longer accustomed after their experience in private duty. They were again subject to the supervision of nursing superintendents and head nurses as well as the authority of hospital superintendents and physicians. Wages were typically low and the hours long; jobs were insecure and sometimes temporary, varying with the hospital's census [82].

Although the 1930s witnessed the rise of the labor movement among industrial workers, resistance to conditions on hospital wards was mainly informal. As Reverby has argued, graduate nurses had been socialized to accept the obligation to care without consideration of the rights that might accompany that obligation [83]. Few nurses belonged to unions, and throughout the 1930s the ANA and nursing leaders avoided involving the occupation with organized labor. As indicated earlier, in promoting the hiring of nurses, leaders advertised the availability of graduate nurses at low wages and even suggested that as professionals, they would be more easily managed. Still, graduate nurses did not simply accommodate existing arrangements on the wards. They would not be treated like apprentices and sometimes engaged in informal acts of resistance, refusing heavy assignments and engaging in absenteeism to oppose working conditions.

During this period the staff nurse's role was particularly unsettled. As Davies states,

> the depression created conditions conducive to the employment of trained nurses in the hospital, but it did not generate a distinctively defined role for them in that institution. Trained nurses were integrated into hospitals at the point where their own position was an extremely weak one. Unorganized as staff nurses, varied in their

knowledge and skills and economically disadvantaged, they could
not begin to specify their own work content [84].

In accepting hospital employment graduate nurses entered institutions in which either apprentices or untrained attendants had
predominated. With their experience in private duty, graduate
nurses were used to individualized work and the complete care
of patients. They had not worked in a collective labor process
since their years in apprenticeship training, and they had never
worked with workers whose occupational status was below their own.
Their efforts to specify a distinctive work jurisdiction on hospital wards
was soon disrupted by World War II and the introduction of auxiliary
workers.

Nursing's transformation from private duty to hospital employment
involved not simply the employment of graduate nurses and the
gradual displacement of apprentices, but the inclusion of nurses' aides
and practical nurses, creating a new occupational hierarchy and
division of labor inside hospitals. Nurses' aides were introduced beginning in the late 1930s when several thousand were trained by the
Works Progress Administration. However, in the 1940s their numbers
soared. Approximately 150,000 were trained by the Red Cross to staff
hospital wards during World War II, when many graduate nurses left
to serve in the military [85]. Hospitals soon began training aides
themselves. In addition, many practical nurses who had worked
in private duty also sought institutional employment. Some received
formal training in schools for practical nurses, which would become
common with the credentialing and licensing of practical nurses during
the 1950s. When graduate nurses returned to civilian hospitals after
the war, practical nurses and nurses' aides had become a critical
part of hospital staffing. In the next chapter, I discuss how administrators attempted to organize a stratified work force into cooperating
work groups.

NOTES

1. For recent social histories of nursing, see Philip A. Kalisch and Beatrice J.
   Kalisch, *The Advance of American Nursing,* 2nd ed. (Boston: Little, Brown
   and Company, 1986); Barbara Melosh, *The Physician's Hand: Work Cul-
   ture and Conflict in American Nursing* (Philadelphia: Temple University
   Press, 1982); Susan M. Reverby, *Ordered to Care* (Cambridge: Cambridge
   University Press, 1987).

2. Kathleen Cannings and William Lazonick, "The Development of the Nursing Labor Force in the United States: A Basic Analysis," in *Organization of Health Workers and Labor Conflict,* ed. Samuel Wolfe (Amityville, N.Y.: Baywood, 1978), table 6.

3. See, Melosh, *Physician's Hand,* chap. 2; Reverby, *Ordered to Care,* chap. 4; Jo Ann Ashley, *Hospitals, Paternalism, and the Role of the Nurse* (New York: Teachers College Press, 1976).

4. May Ayres Burgess, *Nurses, Patients, and Pocketbooks* (New York: Committee on the Grading of Nursing Schools, 1928), 434.

5. Ashley, *Hospitals, Paternalism, and the Role of the Nurse,* 31.

6. May Ayres Burgess, "Some Problems in Grading our Schools of Nursing," *Trained Nurse and Hospital Review* 77 (Nov. 1926): 507-509. Also, Kalisch and Kalisch, *Advance of American Nursing,* 390.

7. For further discussion of the characteristics of training schools, see Josephine Goldmark, *Nursing and Nursing Education in the United States* (New York: Macmillan, 1923), chap. 12. Also see sources in n. 3.

8. Graded training is discussed in Goldmark, *Nursing and Nursing Education,* 298-301. On the origin of the case method among nursing educators, see Reverby, *Ordered to Care,* chap. 8 and pp. 255-256, nn. 53, 68. For further discussion of the case and functional methods, see Carl Joiner and Gwen Marram van Servellen, *Job Enrichment in Nursing* (Rockville, Md.: Aspen, 1984), chap. 2 and 3.

9. Goldmark provided an example of graded training on a twenty-seven bed ward staffed with five apprentices that in fact combined both case and task methods. The most senior apprentice was assigned less acutely ill patients along with ward management duties, including accompanying doctors on their rounds. In other instances, this nurse might have been assigned the administration of medications or charting for all patients. Another advanced apprentice in her second year was assigned the five most acutely ill patients, and a junior apprentice with one year of experience was assigned six patients, including some that were acutely ill and others that were convalescent patients. However, two apprentices in their first year were not only assigned seven convalescent patients each but housekeeping tasks for the entire ward, relieving senior apprentices of this routine work. Goldmark, *Nursing and Nursing Education,* 299-303.

10. Ibid., 303-307.

11. See Susan Reverby, "The Search for the Hospital Yardstick: Nursing and the Rationalization of Hospital Work," in *Health Care in America: Essays in Social History,* ed. Susan Reverby and David Rosner (Philadelphia: Temple University Press, 1979), 206-225.

12. Ibid., 209; also Reverby, *Ordered to Care,* 151.

13. As Reverby acknowledges, the application of scientific management to hospitals was "more rhetoric than reality" before World War II. See "Search for the Hospital Yardstick," 218-219.

14. Ibid., 210.
15. See Reverby, *Ordered to Care*, chap. 3 and 8.
16. For discussions of gender and authority within this institutional context, see Ashley, *Hospitals, Paternalism, and the Role of the Nurse.*
17. Quoted in Susan Reverby, "Re-forming the Hospital Nurse" in *The Sociology of Health and Illness*, ed. Peter Conrad and Rochelle Kern (New York: St. Martin's Press, 1981), 222.
18. See Reverby, *Ordered to Care*, chap. 3.
19. Ibid.
20. Lynn Y. Weiner, *From Working Girl to Working Mother: The Female Labor Force in the United States, 1880-1980* (Chapel Hill: University of North Carolina Press, 1985), 14; David M. Katzman, *Seven Days A Week: Women and Domestic Service in Industrializing America* (Urbana: University of Illinois Press, 1981), table A-3.
21. Melosh, *Physician's Hand*, 43.
22. Reverby, "Search for the Hospital Yardstick," 212.
23. Burgess, *Nurses, Patients, and Pocketbooks*, 137-141.
24. May Ayres Burgess, "Nurses, Patients, and Pocketbooks," a paper read at the Annual Convention of Nursing Organizations, Louisville, Kentucky, 7 June 1928, *Bulletin of the American Hospital Association* 2 (July 1928): 300-301; Quoted in Reverby, "Search for the Hospital Yardstick," 212.
25. Burgess, *Nurses, Patients, and Pocketbooks*, 440.
26. Burgess, "Nurses, Patients, and Pocketbooks," 300-301; Reverby, "Search for the Hospital Yardstick," 212.
27. Burgess, *Nurses, Patients, and Pocketbooks*, 441.
28. Ashley, *Hospitals, Paternalism, and the Role of the Nurse*, 27.
29. For the characteristics of total institutions, see Erving Goffman, *Asylums: Essays on the Social Situation of Mental Patients and Other Inmates* (Garden City, N.Y.: Doubleday-Anchor, 1961), 3-12. For further discussion of institutional control in the apprenticeship system, see Melosh, *Physician's Hand*, chap. 2.
30. Burgess, *Nurses, Patients, and Pocketbooks*, 439.
31. Melosh, *Physician's Hand*, 50.
32. Temple Burling, Edith M. Lentz, and Robert N. Wilson, *The Give and Take in Hospitals* (New York: G. P. Putnam's Sons, 1956), 98-99.
33. See Goffman, *Asylums*, 171-320.
34. Melosh, *Physician's Hand*, chap. 2.
35. Burgess, *Nurses, Patients, and Pocketbooks*, 250-251.
36. Weiner, *From Working Girl to Working Mother*, table 1.
37. Burgess, *Nurses, Patients, and Pocketbooks*, 528.
38. Ibid., 438.
39. For further discussion of the advantages of private duty nursing, see Melosh, *Physician's Hand*, chap. 3.

40. I discuss this view extensively in chap. 5.
41. David Wagner, "The Proletarianization of Nursing in the United States, 1932-1946," *International Journal of Health Services* 10(2) (1980): 271-290.
42. Melosh, *Physician's Hand,* chap. 2, 3 and pp. 204-205. Melosh's work is itself ambiguous on the craft status of nurses. On the one hand she suggests that nurses had strong craft traditions, and on the other she discusses many of the constraints on graduate nurses' practice of their craft. I have benefitted greatly from her book and draw upon it to emphasize the weakness of graduate nurses' occupational autonomy and control over their work. For additional insightful comments on the ambiguity of graduate nurses' position in private duty, see Reverby, *Ordered to Care,* chap. 6.
43. Theodore Caplow, *The Sociology of Work* (New York: McGraw-Hill, 1954), 48, 246; Katzman, *Seven Days a Week.*
44. Committee on the Grading of Nursing Schools, *Nursing Schools Today and Tomorrow* (New York: privately published, 1934), 45. Quoted in Ashley, *Hospitals, Paternalism, and the Role of the Nurse,* 67. For data on number of graduate nurses, see Cannings and Lazonick, "Development of the Nursing Labor Force," table 6.
45. For discussions of private duty during the 1920s and 1930s, see Melosh, *Physician's Hand,* chap 3; Susan Reverby, " 'Something Besides Waiting': The Politics of Private Duty Nursing Reform in the Depression," in *Nursing History: New Perspectives, New Possibilities,* ed. Ellen Condliffe Legemann (New York: Teachers College Press, Columbia University, 1983), 133-156; Reverby, *Ordered to Care,* chap. 6 and 9.
46. On the limitations of licensing and credentialing, see Melosh, *Physician's Hand,* 39-40. For a discussion of the importance of market shelters, see Eliot Freidson, "Occupational Autonomy and Labor Market Shelters," in *Varieties of Work,* ed. Phillis L. Stewart and Muriel G. Cantor (Beverly Hills: Sage, 1982), 39-60.
47. Burgess, *Nurses, Patients, and Pocketbooks,* 346-348.
48. Quotations in Ashley, *Hospitals, Paternalism, and the Role of the Nurse,* 62-63.
49. Burgess, *Nurses, Patients, and Pocketbooks,* 280.
50. Ibid., 191-192.
51. On relations with registries, see Burgess, *Nurses, Patients, and Pocketbooks,* 71-73; Melosh, *Physician's Hand,* 81-82; Wagner, "Proletarianization of Nursing," 275.
52. Burgess, *Nurses, Patients, and Pocketbooks,* 137-148.
53. Ibid., 289.
54. Goldmark, *Nursing and Nursing Education,* 14-16; Burgess, *Nurses, Patients, and Pocketbooks,* 467-470.

55. For further discussion, see Reverby, *Ordered to Care,* 95-105.

56. Kalisch and Kalisch, *Advance of American Nursing,* 219.

57. For further discussion of household constraints in private duty nursing, see Melosh, *Physician's Hand,* chap. 3; Reverby, *Ordered to Care,* chap. 6.

58. Melosh, *Physician's Hand,* chap. 3; Reverby, *Ordered to Care,* chap 6. Physicians reported a strong demand for practical nurses specifically because they would engage in housework in addition to nursing. See Burgess, *Nurses, Patients, and Pocketbooks,* 152.

59. Esther Lucile Brown, "Nursing and Patient Care," in *The Nursing Profession: Five Sociological Essays,* ed. Fred Davis (New York: John Wiley and Sons, 1966), 182.

60. Melosh, *Physician's Hand,* 106.

61. Ibid., 120, 152.

62. Ibid., 140-141.

63. Burgess, *Nurses, Patients, and Pocketbooks,* 534.

64. Ibid., 197-200; Melosh, *Physician's Hand,* 92.

65. Melosh, *Physician's Hand,* 109.

66. Reverby, "Re-forming the Hospital Nurse," 223.

67. Reverby, *Ordered to Care,* 103, 183. Burgess reported that whereas 46% of graduate nurses worked in the hospital as specials, 37% continued to work in the home, and 17% did both. *Nurses, Patients, and Pocketbooks,* table 37.

68. Melosh, *Physician's Hand,* 99.

69. Ibid.

70. Burgess, *Nurses, Patients, and Pocketbooks,* 311-313. On the decline of private duty, see Reverby, "Something Besides Waiting."

71. Melosh, *Physician's Hand,* 107; Anselm Strauss, "The Structure and Ideology of American Nursing: An Interpretation," in *The Nursing Profession: Five Sociological Essays,* ed. Fred Davis, 99.

72. Mary M. Roberts, *American Nursing: History and Interpretation* (New York: Macmillan, 1961), 223. Also, see Reverby, *Ordered to Care,* 176-179.

73. Kalisch and Kalisch, *Advance of American Nursing,* 462, 479.

74. Burgess, *Nurses, Patients, and Pocketbooks,* 431.

75. Wagner, "Proletarianization of Nursing," 277.

76. Reverby, "Search for the Hospital Yardstick," 216.

77. Reverby, *Ordered to Care,* 190.

78. Ibid., 188.

79. American Nurses' Association, *Facts About Nursing, 1941* (New York: American Nurses' Association, 1941), 35.

80. Roberts, *American Nursing,* 286.

81. Reverby, "Search for the Hospital Yardstick," 217; Kalisch and Kalisch, *Advance of American Nursing,* 458; Wagner, "Proletarianization of Nursing," 278.

82. See Melosh, *Physician's Hand,* chap. 5; Reverby, *Ordered to Care,* chap. 10; Wagner, "Proletarianization of Nursing," 280-284.
83. Reverby, *Ordered to Care,* 199-207.
84. Celia Davies, "The Regulation of Nursing Work: An Historical Comparison of Britain and the U.S.A.," in *Research in the Sociology of Health Care: A Research Annual,* ed. Julius A. Roth (Greenwood, Conn.: JAI Press, 1982), 2: 142-143.
85. Kalisch and Kalisch, *Advance of American Nursing,* 504, 556-557.

CHAPTER 4

Stratified Workers, Subdivided Work: Team Nursing

In this chapter I examine "team nursing," the organization of nursing labor that originated in the late 1940s and that prevailed on hospital wards throughout the postwar expansion of the 1950s and 1960s. As hospitals employed graduate nurses, practical nurses, and nurses' aides, administrators were confronted with the problem of how to effectively organize these stratified workers into cooperating work groups. Studies commissioned by industry elites recommended that the ranks of nurses be clearly differentiated through credentialing and licensing. RNs and auxiliary nurses would then be assigned different tasks corresponding with their level of credentialing and be integrated into teams under the supervision of RNs.

Contrary to the recent claim that team nursing deprofessionalized the occupation, in the immediate postwar decades, the stratification of the work force and the differentiation of tasks was promoted as consistent with professionalization. This view was held by industry and nursing elites and supported by sociological studies funded by the American Nurses' Association (ANA) to determine how nursing "functions" or tasks were actually being organized. Nevertheless, in focusing on occupational interests and professionalization, these studies neglected managerial interests and the distinction between the occupational division of labor and the division of labor on hospital wards—the labor process. In a reinterpretation of team nursing, I argue that although hospital employment and team nursing were an advance over hospital apprenticeship and private duty, team nursing subordinated RNs in a hospital-based labor process that inhibited as well as promoted professionalization. Team nursing was a complex organization of work that combined aspects of both professional upgrading and proletarianization. Scientific management principles were applied to subdivide work, yet nurses were not deskilled. Rather, tasks were upgraded and RNs assigned overall responsibility for nursing care and the supervision of routine work delegated to practical nurses and nurses' aides. At the same time, RNs remained semiprofessional wage labor subject to exploitation and domination by administrators and physicians. To understand RNs' recent cooperation in the reunification of nursing tasks, it is necessary to see how team nursing failed to resolve difficulties among stratified workers. In closing the chapter, I argue that the problems of team nursing originated in the constraints on rationalizing work rather than in the successful application of scientific management principles, as maintained by advocates of primary nursing and suggested by theories of technical proletarianization.

ORGANIZING A STRATIFIED WORK FORCE

While nurses in the immediate postwar years remembered the severe unemployment of the 1930s and feared another depression, the economy began a long wave of expansion, and the health care industry grew rapidly. The apprenticeship system of labor continued to decline as hospitals, under pressure to upgrade the quality of their training programs, provided more classroom hours and replaced the unpaid labor of apprentices with wage labor. As the industry expanded, hospitals employed available graduate nurses, practical nurses, and nurses' aides, and still complained of a shortage of nursing workers. Moreover, the inclusion of these stratified workers on hospital wards was proceeding with difficulty. As the postwar period began, hospital and nursing administrators faced the dual problem of attracting more nurses to hospital employment and effectively organizing their labor [1].

Two major studies were conducted by nursing and industry elites in the late 1940s in response to this challenge. A report by the Committee on the Function of Nursing was authored by committee chairman Eli Ginzberg (the Ginzberg Report) and a report for the National Nursing Council was written by Esther Lucille Brown (the Brown Report). Both reports addressed the organizational problems confronting hospital and nursing elites and advocated similar solutions [2].

To attract and retain nursing workers, these reports recommended that hospitals improve working conditions. In the late 1940s, the system of apprenticeship labor was not yet completely dismantled, and older nurses continued "perpetuating the stringent system of discipline that prevailed in their student days." In addition, although the length of the workweek had declined significantly, nurses still worked an average of forty-six hours per week, which included shift work as well as work on weekends. Many hospitals still "required their nurses to work 'split shifts,' wherein the working day . . . consisted of two tours of duty, with intervening time off which was not paid for" [3]. While the work load remained heavy, nurses' wages were relatively low.

The major problem, however, was not simply or even primarily one of labor supply. As hospitals employed increasing numbers of RNs, practical nurses, and aides, relations among these workers were troublesome. According to Brown, "No such expansion could have been achieved in a relatively short period of time without many accompanying problems and dissatisfactions. Because the role of nursing had not been well defined following the decline of private duty nursing, and because thousands of graduate nurses had been prepared in weak hospital schools that could give them only narrow technical training, many viewed the introduction of aides and later of practical nurses as a threat to themselves." To preserve their own status, graduate nurses often treated practical nurses and nurses' aides like "scrub women," creating tension on the wards [4].

Difficulties between graduate nurses and auxiliaries resulted not merely from the marginal status of graduate nurses but from the unsettled organization of nursing labor on hospital wards. In organizing work, administrators attempted to use the two formal methods familiar to them: the case and the functional methods. As discussed in the last chapter, the case method assigned the nurse complete care of the patient and was associated with ideal training methods and the individualized care of patients in private duty nursing. In contrast, the functional method was task-oriented and was associated with the application of scientific management principles and the subdivision of work. The task approach had been used in the apprenticeship system to deal with the burden of multiple patient assignments, but with the unpaid labor of apprentices, superintendents had little incentive to systematically apply scientific management principles. With the employment of a stratified work force of wage workers in the postwar period, administrators became increasingly interested in the rationalization of nursing work, yet found the functional method as well as the case method to be inadequate.

The case method assigned the complete care of each patient to an individual nurse, but as in the apprenticeship system, a multiple patient assignment compromised this approach. Moreover, nursing leaders considered the case method inappropriate with a work force that included nonprofessional workers. Although head nurses assigned the more acutely ill patients to RNs and the convalescent patients to auxiliaries, nursing leaders argued that the case method did not provide a means for ensuring that complete nursing care was adequately produced or effectively supervised. Convalescent patients might not require a great deal of technical skill, but nursing leaders believed that a fully trained professional nurse was needed to ensure that the patient's entire nursing needs, including their psychological and emotional needs, were properly attended to. Thus, Eleanor C. Lambertsen, a key figure in the development of team nursing, insisted that "the case method of an over-all pattern of assignment is impossible when services of nonprofessional personnel are utilized for patient care. Total care of patients cannot and should not be assigned to other than the professional nurse" [5].

Behind the concern for appropriate patient care were occupational interests eager to subordinate auxiliary nurses by creating an intraoccupational hierarchy under professional nursing control. Nursing's leaders were not satisfied with a method of assignment that gave nonprofessional nurses responsibility and immediate control over the complete care of their own patients, and were determined to develop a means of organizing work that secured RNs' positions over the growing ranks of nonprofessional nurses on hospital wards.

Task-oriented functional nursing seemed to offer such an opportunity. In this method, the head nurse assigned graduate nurses, practical nurses, and nurses' aides to specific tasks rather than to the complete care of patients. Administrators found this method appealing because of its promise of efficiency and economy [6]. Yet, despite what were believed to be its advantages, functional nursing was considered inadequate as well. Nursing was not machine-paced, like a factory assembly line. The more that individual tasks were separated from general nursing care, the more problematic was nursing's integration, jeopardizing the complete care of patients and creating adverse working conditions [7].

Without a satisfactory method of organizing work, head nurses adapted and combined variations of both methods, but relations among workers remained difficult. In addressing these problems, the Brown and Ginzberg Reports first recommended that stratified nurses be organized in a hierarchical division of labor with clear distinctions in occupational training, credentialing, and licensing. Both reports proposed that the credentialing of graduate nurses be upgraded and that auxiliary nurses be adequately trained in subsidiary programs under professional nursing's control. Each report argued that the graduates of three year hospital diploma schools were not professionally educated. "How could they be when one recalls the narrowness and the poverty of the training provided them? Frequently their competence is no greater than that which should be possessed by the well-prepared practical nurse" [8]. Although both reports were cautious about calling for the elimination of hospital-based schools (the graduates of these programs were still needed to staff hospital wards), Brown and Ginzberg maintained that the title of "professional nurse" should be restricted to registered nurses and in the long run to RNs with baccalaureate degrees from college and university programs. If RNs with less than a baccalaureate degree were needed for an extended period, Brown suggested that hospital schools be replaced by community college programs. Meanwhile, the reports advised that auxiliaries be clearly subordinated to the RN through vocational training and in the case of practical nurses, through licensing as well [9].

Brown and Ginzberg also addressed the problem of how work was to be organized on hospital wards and recommended a similar solution. Just as the occupational division of labor would be organized around clear distinctions in nurses' training and credentialing, the various ranks of nurses would be assigned clearly differentiated tasks or nursing "functions." To offset any tendency toward fragmentation, stratified nurses would be organized into cooperating teams under the supervision of RNs [10]. The "team approach" supposedly combined the advantages of the functional and case methods while overcoming their deficiencies and providing for the exercise of RNs' professional responsibility and the supervision of nonprofessional nurses. According to Ginzberg, the team approach

> does not deny the possibilities inherent in differentiations based on the class of patients or on type of functions, but places its major reliance on the performance of the total nursing mission by a group of nurses in which the essential element is the supervisory

relationship between the registered or professional nurse and the practical nurse [11].

The key to this method was a distinct separation of training and duties, effective supervision, and RNs' professional responsibility for the tasks performed by auxiliary nurses.

> The "team approach" places full responsibility for the planning of the nursing function and the primary responsibility for its proper execution on the most mature and competently trained individual, the professional nurse, and leaves to her the assignment of specific duties among others less competently trained [12].

Similarly, Brown drew upon her studies of other professions to emphasize that RNs' professional tasks would be clearly separated from nonprofessional tasks which could be delegated to auxiliary nurses, and that, at the same time, overall responsibility for nursing care would remain with the RN, the professional nurse [13].

The Ginzberg and Brown Reports were not speculative accounts. Both reports were commissioned by nursing and industry leaders close to actual developments in hospitals and incorporated ideas in circulation among elite groups. A formal differentiation of occupational roles and work jurisdictions soon followed. As Cannings and Lazonick point out,

> by the late 1940s, the general structure of the nursing labor force . . . had clearly taken shape. The hospital had become the primary workplace of the nursing labor force, and the major divisions among nursing workers had been institutionalized by means of educational standards, licensure, job descriptions, and the formation of various occupational organizations [14].

After 1950, registration and licensing were mandatory in most states, and graduate nurses soon uniformly used the title of registered nurse or RN. The nursing profession also gained control over the credentialing and licensing of practical nurses, now known as LPNs (licensed practical nurses). Although nurses' aides were not required to be licensed, they were subordinated through training and job descriptions within nursing departments controlled by RN administrators [15].

The detailed specification of work tasks also proceeded in the immediate years following the Ginzberg and Brown Reports. Both reports called for additional studies of how to organize stratified nurses according to the principles of task differentiation and team integration. Such studies were soon forthcoming, and they included an influential manual by Eleanor Lambertsen that served as a guide for organizing team nursing throughout the 1950s and 1960s [16].

While on the faculty in nursing education at Teachers College, Columbia University, Lambertsen participated in studies to implement what was becoming known as "team nursing." To clearly differentiate nursing tasks Lambertsen divided work along a continuum wherein the most skilled tasks were to be performed by RNs, semiskilled tasks by LPNs, and unskilled tasks by nurses' aides. As professional nurses RNs were responsible for all nursing care, and consequently, for the work produced by auxiliaries. Under the ward head nurse, whose span of direct supervision was greatly reduced, RN "team leaders" would plan patient care and assign nonprofessional tasks to auxiliary workers under their supervision. RNs would interpret physicians' orders, identify the needs of patient, and maintain the nursing care plan (the written document of the care to be produced for each patient) [17].

In contrast to professional nurses, auxiliaries were expected to perform assigned routine tasks. LPNs and nurses' aides received separate training and their work was formally differentiated somewhat, but Lambertsen as well as other nursing leaders considered both occupations ancillary personnel to be subordinated within the nursing team. LPNs were the most threatening to RNs, and efforts were made to clearly restrict this nearest competitor to a subordinate work jurisdiction. Deming had argued that

> practical nurses can be used safely where they can follow standardized routines established by the hospital. . . . They can be used where no new judgement will be required of them and they are not expected to adapt their routines to a patient's changing condition, but to report that condition at once for further orders [18].

Nurses' aides were less threatening to RNs, but Lambertsen indicated that they were expected to limit themselves to "simple observations," to "use the patient's own words," and to "describe rather than interpret." Their work was viewed as requiring only the "common knowledge" needed to perform tasks barely distinguishable from the domestic work that women performed while caring for family members [19].

At the same time that tasks were to be clearly differentiated, auxiliaries would be integrated into cooperating teams under the supervision of RNs. To this end, Lambertsen emphasized a human relations perspective on communication and work group participation that largely contravened the rigid hierarchy being designed. Thus, Lambertsen extolled the nursing team as "more than a reorganization or restructuring of a nursing service. It represents a philosophy of nursing and of patient care as well as a method of organization" [20]. While nursing workers were to perform sharply differentiated tasks legitimized by differential training, skills, and credentialing, team ideology emphasized participation, mutual communication, and team spirit. In actuality, the differentiation of occupations and tasks consolidated RNs' position over auxiliaries. RN team leaders would supervise auxiliaries' performance of routine bedside care tasks, the parameters of which were set by professional nursing.

Lambertsen's guide was soon joined by a proliferation of articles and books on team nursing, which became the principal model for nursing practice as hospitals employed increasing numbers of LPNs and aides and confronted the difficulty of organizing stratified workers into cooperating groups [21]. By 1950, auxiliaries already surpassed the number of RNs on hospital wards. As the industry continued to expand throughout the postwar period, the composition of nursing workers continued to shift toward a greater proportion of auxiliaries, eventually reaching a composition of approximately two-thirds auxiliaries and one-third RNs in the late 1960s and early 1970s [22]. Meanwhile, during the 1950s nursing leaders sponsored studies by social scientists to determine whether nursing was actually being organized in the manner advocated.

TEAM NURSING AS PROFESSIONALIZATION

Some of the most important sociological studies of nursing were conducted in the 1950s as team nursing was being implemented in hospitals across the country. In their drive to professionalize the occupation, nursing leaders and the ANA sponsored over thirty studies of nurses and their work. These studies include important investigations by Habenstein and Christ, Reissman and Rohrer, and other social scientists, providing a wealth of information about the occupation during the team nursing period [23]. Although a number of topics were addressed, including the social characteristics of nurses as well as their roles and career patterns, the purpose of the studies was to determine the way in which nursing tasks or "functions" were actually being performed by a stratified work force of RNs and auxiliaries. Nursing leaders hoped that nurses' work was being organized in a manner that would advance the professionalization of the occupation.

In an invaluable synthesis of the ANA-sponsored studies, Everett Hughes and his associates found that nursing was indeed undergoing a process of task differentiation that corresponded with the team approach advocated by industry and nursing elites. RNs were spending less time in direct patient care and more time in specialized tasks and team supervision, whereas auxiliaries were attending to the routine bedside care.

> In the thousands of details in these surveys, some general trends and conditions are discernable. In the first place, they show unanimously that bedside care is no longer the principal occupation of the professional nurse. . . . To generalize very broadly from the reports today, the professional nurse is chiefly an administrator, organizer and teacher. . . . She will direct a team of student nurses, practical nurses, and . . . aides. Not only has her work become managerial on ward and floor, but also that part which is strictly nursing has become specialized. . . . All the studies tell this story. . . . The care of the person—the bedside, or "touch" tasks, as they are called—is now largely in the hands of auxiliary nurses; and among the several ranks of the auxiliaries this responsibility is, in turn, passed down so that . . . the nurse aide is likely to provide a greater proportion of direct patient care than is the licensed practical nurse [24].

According to Hughes, the differentiation of nursing tasks was characteristic of professionalization. In essays written throughout the 1950s and 1960s, Hughes maintained that other occupations, including teachers, social workers, and librarians, were also reorganizing their work, but he often referred to nursing to illustrate the process [25]. For Hughes, an occupation's social role included "a bundle of tasks" that is reorganized as occupations upgrade their work and responsibilities, delegating less skilled, routine tasks to nonprofessional workers. In doing so, the professionalizing occupation seeks a monopoly over higher-level tasks while curtailing its involvement in tasks it considers less than professional. Hughes wrote that "the process of turning an art and an occupation into a profession often includes the attempt to drop certain tasks to some other kind of worker. And this is exactly what is happening to the nursing profession" [26]. As medical knowledge and technology advanced, a more complex division of labor was developing, and RNs were upgrading their tasks while delegating routine and dirty work to LPNs and nurses' aides.

Other sociologists had arrived at similar conclusions. For example, in an empirical study sponsored by the ANA, Reissman and Rohrer discussed the differentiation of nursing as follows:

> Paralleling . . . [the] reassignment of technical functions from physician to nurse is the delegation to aides and attendants of functions once performed exclusively by the nurse, although the nurse still maintains a right to engage in these activities when she chooses. These functional changes have occurred as a result of the growth of hospital organization and as a result of the increased technology required in caring for the sick. Hospitals have increased in size and complexity. Specialization at all levels of work has increased [27].

And, as mentioned earlier, Brown had also completed studies of other professions and argued that differentiating tasks was characteristic of professional upgrading, proposing that nursing follow a similar path.

This view of occupational differentiation and the growing complexity of the division of labor has become a part of contemporary sociological theories of professionalization. In a recent and celebrated study of professions, Andrew Abbott has emphasized that professionalizing occupations compete with one another over work jurisdictions and typically claim exclusive jurisdiction over tasks requiring greater expertise while delegating routine work formerly within the occupation's jurisdiction to subordinate occupations, creating hierarchical divisions of labor that include paraprofessional workers [28].

Professionalization does not necessarily occur smoothly. Hughes emphasized that the upgrading of occupations creates "social drama," as the process involves not simply reassigning tasks but reorganizing occupational roles in which people are personally invested. In the case of nursing, many RNs were attached to the bedside role and were reluctant to give up some of the routine tasks. Although RNs were still responsible for performing the more technical tasks, assuming responsibility for overall nursing care pulled them away from a continuous presence at the bedside. At the same time, LPNs and aides were likely to resent being assigned to the bulk of the occupation's "dirty work" [29].

To complicate matters further, Hughes found that in practice the boundaries between work jurisdictions were often blurred and that tasks overlapped extensively. Workers who believed that a particular task fell within their occupational jurisdiction were often not the only workers to actually perform the task. Thus, RNs, LPNs, and nurses' aides competed over work jurisdictions. Practical nurses claimed that they could do everything that RNs could do as well as tasks that aides could not. Meanwhile, nurses' aides claimed they could do everything that LPNs could do. Actually, tasks overlapped at the same time that a larger formal differentiation of work was taking place. Thus, RNs might perform lower-level tasks, but they were likely to view such tasks as properly belonging to auxiliary nurses, claiming upgraded tasks as an exclusive professional jurisdiction [30].

Task differentiation and the delegation of routine work downward was accompanied by efforts to institutionalize corresponding levels of status and rewards. Hughes and his colleagues indicated that the hierarchy that resulted created a caste system in which "the formal status of the newest professional nurse is superior to that of the most competent and experienced practical nurse" [31]. RNs attempted to distinguish themselves from auxiliaries by using symbols and titles to indicate their higher status. They believed that auxiliaries should not be allowed to wear the same uniform and excluded them from activities associated with a higher occupational status. Typically, LPNs and aides were barred from "report" at the beginning and end of shift, restricted from access to doctors' orders, and not allowed to chart in patients' records. Status distinctions were also reinforced by patterns of social interaction within the hospital. RNs and auxiliaries often associated separately during meal breaks, and some hospitals even had separate dining areas [32].

Because Hughes' view of professionalization generally supported the aspirations of nursing leaders, in their desire to upgrade the status of the occupation, nursing leaders were willing to overlook the more critical aspects of his interpretation. At certain points in his writing, Hughes acknowledged that the outcome of nursing's professionalization appeared different from that of the elite professions. To achieve professional success in nursing required that RNs leave bedside nursing behind. And, even then, occupational mobility was limited. As Hughes observed, nurses

> have titles, each containing the word "nurse," and all begin with an education in the "touch" tasks, as if they were all going to have identical work. For the name "nursing," as we have seen, has become a catchall for an array of occupations including among them administration, supervision and teaching, in which the road to advancement leads of necessity away from the tending of the sick, and for women, for the most part at present, down a blind alley [33].

Hughes was one of the early occupational sociologists to link problems of professionalization to gender, noting that "perhaps it is no accident that certain of the professions—nursing, schoolteaching, social work and library work are among them—in which success requires abdication from the original commitment, are women's worlds" [34].

Despite such comments, Hughes did not alter his prevailing argument that task differentiation had professionalized nursing. In numerous essays Hughes used the example of nursing to illustrate the professionalization of occupations [35]. Furthermore, Hughes was convinced that the entire process was unlikely to be reversed.

> The practical nurse and the nurse aide, often spoken of as temporary, are certainly permanent members of the hospital team. . . . The occupational standard of living, if one may call it that, of the professional nurse has risen so much that she is unlikely to wish to have back *all* her old tasks. Hence when, if ever, the division of labor in hospital nursing is stabilized, we can be sure that it will recognize a variety of ranks of nurse [36].

As Hughes indicated, a dedifferentiation of nursing tasks would be extraordinary. Nevertheless, such a reversal would occur with the implementation of "primary nursing" in the 1970s and 1980s. From Hughes' perspective, which as I have pointed out is well established in sociological theories of professionalization, reunifying tasks would deprofessionalize the occupation as RNs would resume routine tasks formerly delegated to nonprofessional workers. Yet, with the advent of primary nursing, a new generation of nursing leaders would claim the reverse, that team nursing had actually deprofessionalized nursing, and that a reunification of tasks would reprofessionalize the occupation. I will discuss primary nursing in the next chapter. Meanwhile, in a reinterpretation of team nursing I discuss its complexity, the interests that must be taken into account in understanding its development, and the contradictions that would lead rank and file RNs to later embrace primary nursing, even though nursing leaders' goal of professionalization would remain elusive.

A REINTERPRETATION OF TEAM NURSING

In reinterpreting team nursing I do not challenge Hughes' documentation of the major trend revealed by the empirical studies of the 1950s: that RNs' work was being upgraded through task differentiation and the delegation of routine bedside care to auxiliary nurses. However, I argue that team nursing cannot be understood simply by focusing on occupational interests and professionalization. Whereas Hughes linked the differentiation of nursing tasks with the occupational division of labor and professionalization, I will distinguish between the occupational division of labor and the division of labor on hospital wards, arguing that team nursing failed to fully professionalize nursing and was a subordinate labor process that incorporated managerial as well as occupational interests. In neglecting this distinction, Hughes ignored the political economy of work and provided no explanation as to why hospital administrators found team nursing to their benefit [37]. Furthermore, I will also emphasize the distinction between nursing leaders' interest in professionalization and the realities of ward labor for staff nurses. Although Hughes was interested in what was happening on hospital wards, in neglecting the conceptual distinction between the occupational division of labor and the labor process, he provided no basis for understanding why rank and file RNs became dissatisfied with what appeared to be professional upgrading. To understand team nursing and the reunification of tasks that would occur with primary nursing, it is necessary to consider both managerial and occupational interests as well as the contradictions that team nursing posed for staff nurses on hospital wards.

The Limits of Professionalization

Although nursing leaders hoped that team nursing would professionalize the occupation, RNs were unlikely to attain full professional status. In contrast to the elite professions, nursing had the misfortune of being subordinate both to a dominant profession and to the bureaucratic authority of hospital administrators.

As we have seen, physicians' dominance over nurses preceded RNs' employment in hospitals and flourished in the apprenticeship system, when nurses were even required to stand as doctors entered hospital wards. The social deference shown physicians lessened with the decline of apprenticeship labor as employed nurses could not be treated in the same manner as students subject to hospital and training school authoritarianism. Nevertheless, in the immediate postwar period, physicians' position over subordinate occupations was consolidated rather than challenged. In a study completed in the late 1960s, Freidson discussed physicians' professional dominance over an extensive paramedical division of labor. Freidson emphasized that the occupational division of labor in health care was "an organized social structure" distinct from bureaucratic organization and ordered "by professional rather than by administrative authority" [38]. RNs occupied a position subordinate to physicians but superior to other paramedical workers. Thus, although nurses were acquiring some of the formal characteristics of a profession, the dominance of medicine ensured that nursing would remain subordinate.

> An aggressive occupation like nursing can have its own schools for training, can control licensing boards in many instances, and can have its own "service" in hospital, in this way giving the appearance of formal, state-supported, and departmental autonomy, but the work which its members perform remains subject to the order of another occupation. . . . As the case of the nursing shows, those paramedical occupations which are ranged round the physician cannot fail to be subordinate in authority and responsibility and, so long as their work remains medical in character, cannot gain occupational autonomy no matter how intelligent and aggressive its leadership. To attain the autonomy of a profession, the paramedical occupation must control a fairly discrete area of work that can be separated from the main body of medicine and that can be practiced without routine contact with or dependence on medicine. Few if any of the present paramedical occupations deal with such potentially autonomous areas [39].

Furthermore, in contrast to Hughes, Freidson suggested that the differentiation of nursing tasks could not elevate RNs to professional standing. Rather, nurses were "creating a paranursing hierarchy within the paramedical hierarchy" [40].

The prospect of RNs' professionalization was also constrained by the work setting. Hospitals had acquired bureaucratic features before nurses were widely employed in them, but, as discussed earlier, the apprenticeship system relied upon a direct form of personal authority and supervision. With the employment of a stratified work force, bureaucratic control over nurses' work was widely established during the team nursing period. Formal rules and procedures replaced the arbitrary authority of hospital and nursing superintendents, specifying the tasks assigned to various levels of nursing personnel. Thus, unlike the medical profession, which Scott considered an "autonomous professional organization" because physicians' activities were controlled by the medical staff, the nursing profession was "heteronomous" in that RNs were subject to greater administrative authority, limiting their occupational autonomy. Constrained both by bureaucratic control and by physicians' professional dominance, throughout the postwar period nursing has for the most part been considered a semiprofession [41].

A Subordinate Labor Process

Although studies of physicians' professional dominance and the bureaucratic context of nursing work help us to understand the constraints on RNs' professionalization, they do not tell us much about the actual organization of nursing work on hospital wards. Furthermore, if we seek to examine variations in the organization of work, it is important to distinguish between the occupational division of labor and the division of labor in nursing production (the labor process). The occupational division of labor does not necessarily dictate the division of labor in particular work processes [42]. In fact, the *occupational* division of labor in nursing has remained constant throughout the postwar period at the same time that the division of labor *on hospital wards* has varied significantly. Thus, prior to implementing team nursing, hospitals sometimes assigned RNs and auxiliaries to different types of patients rather than to differentiated tasks. And, of course, task differentiation has been reversed with the development of primary nursing. The occupational division of labor among nurses continues to exist, but the division of labor in hospital production (the labor process) has been transformed, and auxiliaries displaced to other work sites.

Furthermore, because team nursing was a hospital-based labor process, managerial as well as occupational interests must be taken into account. As I discuss in the next section, team nursing was created by applying scientific management principles to subdivide nursing tasks. Although the application of these managerial tools is usually associated with the deskilling of occupations, in the case of team nursing RNs' tasks and responsibilities were upgraded, providing a basis for the convergence of administrative and occupational interests. Subdividing tasks was consistent with hospitals' economic and managerial interests as well as nursing's interest in shedding nonprofessional, routine tasks. Nevertheless, because nurses' work remained within a subordinate work jurisdiction, RNs failed to attain a fully professional status and remained vulnerable to exploitation and domination by hospital administrators and physicians.

Subdividing Work without Deskilling, Upgrading Work without Professionalization

As team nursing was implemented in the 1950s, scientific management studies proliferated in an effort to rationalize the organization of work that was emerging with the inclusion of RNs and auxiliaries in a common work process. Many studies were initiated by nursing leaders in their efforts to secure RNs' position in hospitals and to upgrade their tasks. Lillian M. Gilbreth, an efficiency expert, served as an advisor to a series of studies, including one by George and Kuehn that summarized the contributions of scientific management to the development of team nursing and conducted a detailed study of how tasks could be differentiated among RNs, LPNs, and nurses' aides. This study included detailed lists of hundreds of tasks, the level of worker to which each task could appropriately be assigned, corresponding personnel policies and even job evaluation forms [43].

Proletarianization theorists usually associate the application of scientific management principles with "technical proletarianization," that is, the deskilling of crafts and professions; in some cases suggesting that this may be the major trend in the organization of work in capitalist societies. Thus, Braverman argued that deskilling would extend to service industries like health care where semiprofessional workers were likely to experience the adversity of a detailed labor process and degraded work. And, as pointed out earlier, in a study specifically of nursing, Wagner argued that with hospital employment and the subdivision of work, RNs lost their autonomy and status as self-employed professionals, becoming proletarianized workers [44].

Although team nursing subdivided nursing tasks through the application of scientific management principles, it did not deskill nurses. As Hughes recognized, RNs' skills and responsibilities were upgraded rather than downgraded. However, while Hughes stressed the occupational division of labor and the professional character of RNs' work by using terms such as "administrator," and "teacher," [45] RNs were actually "team leaders," the first-line supervisors of auxiliary nurses. As Reverby indicates, "time-and-motion studies were used to create a nursing team that divided functions and then assigned them to different level workers, making the RN the foreman of the team" [46]. RNs were assigned the conceptual work of planning and organizing the production of care, the supervision of auxiliaries, and the more skilled tasks, whereas auxiliaries were assigned the routine bedside care tasks and the bulk of what Hughes called "dirty work." Nursing leaders and administrators expected auxiliaries to confine themselves to the execution of these tasks while avoiding interpretation and the exercise of judgment, activities reserved for the professional nurse.

Because RNs' tasks and responsibilities were upgraded, clearly team nursing did not deprofessionalize the occupation. When compared with prior forms of labor, hospital employment and team nursing not only upgraded tasks but created a circumscribed sphere of responsibility and autonomy that did not previously exist [47]. RNs were subordinate to physicians, to be sure, but doctors were only on hospital wards for short periods of time and did not exercise administrative authority over RNs. While RNs were subordinate to hospital administrators and the nursing department hierarchy, as team leaders they were responsible for organizing patient care and for supervising the work of auxiliary nurses. By contrast, in apprenticeship labor the authoritarianism of hospital and nursing superintendents severely limited the autonomy of nurse apprentices. And, although graduate nurses were free of institutional authority in private duty nursing, their autonomy had been seriously compromised by an open labor market and the power of the patient as both client and employer.

Furthermore, in the 1950s and 1960s nursing leaders believed that differentiating tasks and delegating routine work to auxiliaries was consistent with RNs' professional upgrading. As we have seen, sociological studies commissioned by the ANA supported this interpretation. Still, hospital administrators would not have implemented team nursing if they had perceived it as detrimental to their interests. Team nursing was believed to be cost-effective in that, with the differentiation of nursing tasks, management could employ cheaper workers to perform routine work while assigning technical tasks and the supervision of auxiliary workers to RNs. Thus, although the postwar nursing shortage contributed to the hiring of auxiliaries, administrators staffed hospital wards in a manner they believed prudent. Occupational and managerial interests, always potentially disparate, in this case converged. As a result, management did not have to impose a subdivided labor process to gain what were believed to be the benefits of economy and efficiency [48]. Task differentiation and the delegation of routine tasks to auxiliaries was seen both as a means of professionalization and as sound managerial principle.

Nevertheless, just as team nursing subdivided nursing work without deskilling RNs, it upgraded tasks and responsibility without fully professionalizing nursing. As studies of other labor processes have shown, responsibility and autonomy are not characteristic of professional occupations alone. Likewise, proletarianization (exploitation and domination) does not necessarily require deskilling and tight managerial control [49]. Instead, managers, and in this case, an elite profession conceded limited spheres of responsibility and discretion in order to enlist the cooperation of subordinate workers. Team nursing enlarged RNs' skills and responsibilities at the same time that their work remained in a subordinate work jurisdiction consistent with both semiprofessional status and a vulnerability to exploitation and domination.

The Contradictions of Team Nursing

As we have seen, in some ways team nursing appeared to be the ideal solution to the problem of organizing stratified nursing workers on hospital wards, seeming to fulfill both occupational and managerial goals. Nevertheless, the convergence of interests between nursing leaders and administrators was likely to be limited as team nursing failed to elevate RNs to professional positions. Furthermore, the subdivision of work created dissatisfaction among staff nurses on hospital wards. In explaining this dissatisfaction, a new generation of nursing leaders has argued that, rather than upgrade the occupation, the differentiation of nursing tasks destroyed the integrity of professional practice [50]. As pointed out earlier, social histories of nursing sometimes present similar interpretations. Thus, Melosh suggests that the rationalization of work destroyed the craft of nursing, and Wagner argues that scientific management deskilled RNs [51]. Whether identifying nursing as a craft or a profession, such arguments rely on the premise that the rationalization of nursing work was highly successful. In contrast, in the following discussion I argue that the difficulties of team nursing resulted chiefly from the contradictions of and limitations on subdividing work.

As discussed earlier, team nursing was meant to overcome the difficulties that resulted from the employment of a stratified work force on hospital wards. It was designed to do so by clearly differentiating nursing tasks, integrating RNs and auxiliaries into cooperating teams, and assigning RNs responsibility for the work performed by nonprofessional workers. Nevertheless, although an advance over prior forms of nursing labor, team nursing contained organizational contradictions that generated problems for practicing nurses. First, the effort to clearly differentiate nursing tasks divided workers as well. This might not have created as great a difficulty if differentiated tasks were grounded in clear functional differences between workers. However, and this is the second point, tasks not only overlapped, auxiliaries were able to effectively substitute for RNs, a problem that could not be resolved through a formal division of labor or negotiation of occupational jurisdictions because the exigencies of the labor process required that work jurisdictions be continuously violated, and because RNs were vulnerable to substitution by nonprofessional workers. This not only undermined the professionalization of RNs' work but threatened their control over auxiliary workers. Third, auxiliaries' proximity to patients empowered them and created a competing experience of responsibility that further interfered with RNs' control over nursing work and complicated their accountability to physicians and administrators for the nursing care auxiliaries produced. I support this reinterpretation with evidence from nursing studies completed in the 1950s as well as insights gained through unstructured interviews with nurses at Pacific Hospital who had experienced both team and primary nursing.

Subdivided Work, Divided Workers

The effort to clearly differentiate nursing tasks by assigning RNs to conceptual and supervisory work and auxiliaries to routine bedside care formally divided tasks, but it also divided nursing workers. This produced a corresponding consciousness among RNs and auxiliaries that reflected as well as created difficulties on the wards. Throughout the team nursing period these difficulties could not be resolved, hence they tended to undermine team integration.

Although RNs viewed auxiliaries as members of inferior occupations, their perception of auxiliaries was itself contradictory. On the one hand, RNs commonly believed that auxiliaries were not responsible or dedicated. They could not be trusted, did not work conscientiously, and required close supervision. On the other hand, RNs also complained that auxiliaries were excessively ambitious, did not stay in their place, and engaged in tasks they were not supposed to be doing [52].

Auxiliaries were in a difficult position as their inferiority was structured into the work process by the subdivision of labor. RN team leaders assigned routine tasks to auxiliaries and then evaluated their performance. Because auxiliaries could not claim to be professional nurses, their occupational inferiority legitimized restricting them to routine and dirty work, barring them from conceptualizing the work to be performed or interpreting the needs and responses of patients. Any effort to engage in tasks that formally belonged to the professional nurse could be viewed as overstepping an appropriate occupational role.

Auxiliary nurses also held derogatory views of RNs. LPNs and aides commonly felt that they did all the "real" work. RNs processed doctors' orders, made entries in patients' charts, and maintained the nursing care plans while auxiliaries performed the bulk of bedside care: making beds, emptying bedpans, giving baths, passing meal trays, and doing a variety of other tasks essential to patient care. Habenstein and Christ conveyed the following remarks of a practical nurse whose experience illustrates the problems that sometimes occurred.

> Only this morning, I put one of my patients on the pan and before I could get him off I was sent down to get the linens. I was gone about twenty minutes since they didn't have things counted out or the bed bundles made, and while I was gone the poor man had his light on for at least fifteen minutes and nobody came to unpan him. There were two registered nurses at the station who weren't doing anything, and either one of 'em could have unpanned him. He was *so* weak when I finally got him off. He was nervous, and upset, and mad, *and so was I!* [53].

Nurses at Pacific Hospital confirmed that auxiliaries commonly believed RNs were able to avoid the drudgery of nursing while LPNs and nurses' aides did all the work. As one LPN confided, "RNs had it easy. They didn't have to do the bedside care." A nurses' aide conveyed that "RNs wanted to tell you everything, but you couldn't tell them anything" [54]. Some RN informants were also candid about their relations with auxiliaries:

> Well basically we would tell them what to do. They resented it. They acted like we had it easy, just giving meds, making assignments, doing special procedures and charting. They had to do the routine bedside care, and most of it is routine—giving baths, passing meal trays, emptying bedpans. It got so they would draw the line on other tasks we would ask them to do once they got their work done. You could not rely on them and some were just lazy, I guess.

Because of the difficulties between RNs and auxiliaries, nursing administrators at Pacific and other hospitals established formal job descriptions in an attempt to further demarcate tasks. Bureaucratic rules supplemented RNs' supervision and specified what tasks were to be done and which category of worker was to do them. Administrators hoped such rules would lessen tensions on the wards by reducing RNs' need to repeat directives, and at the same time, provide a basis for job evaluations [55]. However, bureaucratic rules also contributed to the problems of team nursing. In actuality, nurses' tasks could not be clearly differentiated, RNs were vulnerable to substitution by auxiliaries, and the demands of the work process often required RNs to violate rules in order to get the work done.

Overlapping Tasks and Substitution

While the effort to differentiate nursing tasks divided workers and undermined the integration of the nursing team, in practice, tasks overlapped extensively. In daily activities on hospital wards, both RNs and auxiliaries often participated in one another's assigned work. RNs were responsible for performing the more skilled technical tasks and for team administration, but they also engaged in many routine tasks. Some RNs closely identified with the traditional nursing role at the bedside. Others felt they needed to stay more in contact with patients in order to properly supervise auxiliaries. In some cases team leaders performed such tasks to facilitate team integration, demonstrating to auxiliaries that they were not above engaging in such work. However, the exigencies of the work process—staffing problems, the work load, and patients' needs—often forced RNs to perform "nonprofessional" tasks. As an RN at Pacific Hospital explained, "What could you do when you were short on staff, very busy, or a doctor walked onto the ward and wanted something done, but it really was a task assigned to auxiliary nurses?" In other situations, the RN might go into a patient's room to perform a technical task such as starting an intravenous medication, and the patient might indicate that they wanted the bedpan. "You certainly couldn't say, 'wait until the nurses' aide gets back!'"

RNs' participation in the work of LPNs and nurses' aides was more a threat to RNs than to auxiliaries. By performing tasks assigned to auxiliary nurses, RNs subverted the formal rules that had been established to differentiate professional from nonprofessional work. To avoid weakening their work jurisdiction, RNs refused to acknowledge such tasks as part of their regular or formally assigned duties, yet continued to engage in this work as they deemed necessary [56].

The most threatening type of overlap, however, was auxiliaries' substitution for RNs. In addition to performing the bulk of routine tasks, auxiliaries engaged in many tasks formally assigned to the professional nurse. In discussing task overlap Hughes emphasized jurisdictional disputes; however, auxiliaries' substitution for RNs resulted largely from the exigencies of the labor process. Hospital budgets were always limited, and managerial interest in lower labor costs usually meant fewer RNs and more auxiliaries. As a result, to meet patients' needs and the demands of a work load imposed by physicians and administrators, team leaders delegated unauthorized tasks to auxiliaries. In some cases, they trained auxiliaries to do the work. However, RNs were also vulnerable to substitution. In many cases auxiliaries already knew what to do and used knowledge they had assimilated through their own experience and observations on the wards [57].

Throughout the team nursing period, RNs found it difficult to monopolize a set of professional tasks that could not be performed by less credentialed workers. The link between RNs' credentialing and work requirements was weak, leading Caplow to point out in the 1950s that "in the absence of fully qualified personnel, untrained . . . nurses . . . are readily substituted" [58]. The implications of Caplow's comments received little attention until two decades later when Margaret Levi discussed in greater detail the vulnerability of RNs to substitution. Although team nursing was then in decline, Levi argued that auxiliaries' substitution made RNs "functionally redundant," undermining their professionalization and even allowing management to staff with nonprofessional workers during RN strikes [59]. While Levi illustrated RNs' functional redundancy through auxiliaries' substitution on hospital wards during the 1976 RN strike in Seattle, RNs at Pacific Hospital had suffered the same indignity during the 1974 strike in the San Francisco Bay area [60]. Many still had bitter memories of their replacement by auxiliaries, yet acknowledged that in normal daily activities on the wards, auxiliaries' substitution facilitated getting the work done and was often necessary to keep up with the demands of patient care. In many instances it made more sense for team leaders to delegate a professional task to an experienced LPN. As one former team leader at Pacific Hospital confided, "the task may belong to RNs, but what would you do if the only one available to do it was an LPN, and she was more experienced anyway?"

While taking advantage of auxiliaries' ability to substitute, RNs often felt ambivalent doing so. Delegating tasks that fell within their own jurisdiction relieved RNs of an immediate problem, but they resented having to delegate such tasks. Auxiliaries' substitution for RNs undercut the legitimacy of task differentiation and RNs' claim to a higher occupational status. To protect their work jurisdiction, RNs refused to allow auxiliaries to claim more advanced tasks as legitimate areas of work. However, this created further problems because once auxiliaries performed these tasks, their formal restriction to less skilled, routine work seemed arbitrary. The LPN or aide "was understandably reluctant to step back to a more narrow range of activities. She 'knew' how to do the higher prestige task, but her knowledge was considered illegitimate" [61].

Auxiliaries' ability to substitute also contributed to RNs' derogatory views of them. On the one hand auxiliaries often took pride in acquiring new skills or in the opportunity to use skills they had already mastered. On the other hand, whether auxiliaries cooperated or refused to engage in tasks outside their formal work jurisdiction, their response supported RNs' view of their inferiority. When auxiliaries did not readily acquiesce, RNs considered them undedicated or indolent. When auxiliaries did cooperate (which they did for the most part), they demonstrated that they were capable of substituting for RNs and were then accused of being overly ambitious, a criticism that pervaded the work culture.

> You can put me down as not liking practical nurses. Now I know that is probably not right, but I just don't approve of them. They don't stick to the things they should do—they don't stay in their place—first thing you know they are running the place. They wear a uniform and a cap and get all the glory and accept none of the responsibility [62].

Despite tensions between RNs and auxiliaries, overt conflict was usually avoided. All nursing workers had a tendency to blame themselves for problems on the wards. However, because of their positions as team leaders, RNs were able to directly express their frustrations and disapproval of auxiliaries. As Reissman noted, "such expressions of dissatisfaction . . . were a privilege of higher status" [63]. In contrast, auxiliaries often displaced tension onto one another, as an LPN conveys in the following complaints about nurses' aides.

> So far as I am concerned, [they] . . . are not members of the nursing staff, but just learners and part-timers. . . . The orderly who helps us with the heavy work and with catheterizations, and preps and so on is I think of in [sic] the same sort. At least I don't think of him as in the same category with me, but as someone I tell what needs to be done, like a porter or janitor, but just a little bit higher. Now, I think that any of these people, if they apply themselves and study and get more experience can get a license, and become a Licensed Practical Nurse, but, I think until they do prove that they can handle that kind of work they ought to be kept down and doing only the things they are supposed too do. . . . That's why I wear my pin and my sleeve-band, so the patient knows that when I am working with him he is not getting the care of just anybody but the care of a Licensed Practical Nurse [64].

As a result of such tensions, when RNs delegated unauthorized tasks, they also risked losing auxiliaries' cooperation. "In selecting one auxiliary, and not another, to do a professional nurse's task, she risks offending them all and having, from then on, to work with disgruntled assistants" [65].

Furthermore, auxiliaries' substitution complicated RNs' exercise of responsibility. RNs delegated tasks, but they could not delegate their overall responsibility for nursing care. Exercising that responsibility was difficult enough when the delegated task fell within auxiliaries' jurisdiction, but became even more so when the task properly belonged to RNs. As team leaders, RNs were supposed to enforce the rules, but at the same time they violated them in order to get the work done. The RN was then accountable not only for the work of auxiliaries but for the outcome of her own violation of the rules. "Small wonder she is afraid! For she knows that, no matter what happens, the doctor always can say: 'You ought to know that that is no work for a practical nurse!' " [66]. Consequently, in looking back on the experience, an RN at Pacific Hospital stated that "the biggest problem with team nursing was that we were responsible for the work performed by auxiliaries." As I show in the next section, despite the efforts of RNs to meet that obligation, they were often unable to effectively control auxiliaries' work, adding further to RNs' dissatisfaction with team nursing.

Auxiliaries' Empowerment and Competing Responsibility

RNs were formally responsible for all nursing care, yet auxiliaries' propinquity to patients empowered them and provided an experience of responsibility that competed with RNs. While auxiliaries were assigned routine and dirty work, their bedside position in production made them critical to patient care. In a sense the central nursing tasks were not the upgraded tasks assigned to RNs, but the tasks performed by auxiliaries. This was not because auxiliaries' work required a high level of expertise, but because the continual performance of routine tasks provided practical knowledge about patients, their illnesses, and their responses to medical and nursing care. Team leaders were not only dependent upon auxiliaries to perform assigned tasks, they were dependent upon them for information accumulated while at the bedside. Thus, an RN at Pacific Hospital who had worked as a team leader prior to the implementation of primary nursing complained that "auxiliaries knew the patients better than we did."

Although RNs' dominance over auxiliaries was never directly challenged, auxiliaries' propinquity to patients provided a basis for informally resisting or at least limiting the power of team leaders [67]. Practical nurses and nurses' aides could make it difficult for RNs to exercise their responsibility for nursing care by withholding information or by circumventing team leaders. The comments of an RN at Pacific illustrate the problems.

> Sometimes it was as if it were us and them [auxiliaries] and doctors would come on the ward and want to know about their patients. Many times we were not on top of things. The aides and LPNs were doing the bedside care and saw the patients more than we did. The aides might not communicate things to us the way they should have, or we would have to ask them, at times in front of the doctor. When something did not get done and the doctor was angry, the aide could say it wasn't her job [invoking formal rules] or act like we were the ones responsible, and of course we were! You were just stuck in the middle.

Another former team leader continued:

> If you could create a good work situation it would be OK, but it took a lot of effort and many times you simply couldn't. There would be problems. They might not always tell you what you needed to know. Having auxiliary nurses under your supervision and having responsibility for, say, eight patients meant you couldn't possibly keep up with what was going on all the time. You had to rely on the LPNs and aides too much.

Class and racial stratification could accentuate such problems. Thus, the same RN added in a quiet voice that "LPNs and nurses' aides were in the union and some of them were black and that also made it more difficult. It was bad sometimes!" [68].

Auxiliaries' proximity to patients also created an informal experience of responsibility that competed with RNs' authority and formal responsibility for nursing care. This finding is somewhat surprising in that sociological studies from the team nursing period typically view RNs as more committed than auxiliaries. For example, Hughes commented that "a strong sense of responsibility may help separate the professional from the nonprofessional worker." Furthermore, an influential typology of nurses by Habenstein and Christ was based on such a conception. RNs were considered "professionalizers," "traditionalizers," and in some cases "utilizers," but nonprofessional nurses, by definition, were likely to have a utilitarian view of their work [69].

Rather than consider responsibility an exclusive attribute of RNs, it is more accurate to recognize both a formal professional accountability to doctors and administrators and an experience of responsibility at the bedside. RNs were not excluded from the latter because the separation of conceptualization and patient care was never complete. Nonetheless, LPNs and nurses' aides were at the bedside more continuously, and their greater exposure to and familiarity with patients created a quasi-professional consciousness that competed with RNs' formal responsibility for nursing care. In the following account a practical nurse expressed the tensions that could arise.

> The thing that hurts most of all is when the nurse [RN] doesn't do right by the patient. . . . You know, sometimes the aides are a lot closer to the patients than the nurses are. The nurses sit at the desk and write the charts and we are out taking care of the patients and giving them baths and making their beds, so sometimes the patients tell us things. For instance one woman will tell you that she is in very great pain and can she please have something to relieve it. Now maybe you have worked with that patient for many days and you know that she is not the kind to complain if she isn't really in bad pain. Then you go to the nurse and say as nice as you know how to, that Mrs. So and So is in great pain and couldn't she please have something to relieve it. Well, if that nurse turns on you and scolds you for bothering her, or if she says something mean about that patient fussing, it is almost more than you can bear [70].

As such accounts illustrate, auxiliaries could not be limited to routine task performance without concern for the overall care of their patients. Although nonprofessional nurses lacked RNs' credentials and were stuck in dead-end jobs, studies found that, because of their proximity to patients, auxiliaries were actually more service-oriented than RNs [71]. Consequently, it was particularly irritating to RNs when patients identified an auxiliary as their nurse.

To summarize, team nursing upgraded RNs' tasks and responsibilities at the same time that RNs were limited to a semiprofessional position in the medical hierarchy and a subordinate labor process on hospital wards. The effort to rationalize work divided workers and compromised team integration. However, a strict Taylorist approach to nursing was never achieved [72]. RNs' tasks were upgraded rather than downgraded, and the effort to sharply differentiate nursing tasks into professional and nonprofessional categories largely failed. Tasks not only overlapped, but RNs were vulnerable to substitution by auxiliaries, whose proximity to patients empowered them and created a competing experience of responsibility. Although team nursing did not deprofessionalize or deskill nursing, RNs' vulnerability to substitution and the difficulty of exercising responsibility for care produced by auxiliary nurses would lead RNs to cooperate in the implementation of primary nursing and a reunification of nursing tasks in the 1970s and 1980s.

NOTES

1. For a discussion of nursing in the immediate postwar years, see Philip A. Kalisch and Beatrice Kalisch, *The Advance of American Nursing*, 2nd ed. (Boston: Little, Brown and Company,1986), chap. 15, 16.
2. Esther Lucile Brown, *Nursing for the Future: A Report Prepared for the National Nursing Council* (New York: Russell Sage Foundation, 1948); The Committee on the Function of Nursing, *A Program for the Nursing Profession* (New York: MacMillan, 1948). Although the Ginzberg Report is presented as the product of the Committee on the Function of Nursing, I will refer to the report by the name of its principal author.
3. Quotations from Ginzberg, *Program for the Nursing Profession*, 51, 83-84. For more detailed data on economic conditions in nursing in the immediate postwar years, see U.S. Department of Labor, Bureau of Labor Statistics, Bulletin no. 931 (Washington, 1947). Excerpts of this report are included in Bonnie Bullough and Vern Bullough, eds., *Issues in Nursing* (New York: Springer, 1966), 165-171.
4. Esther Lucile Brown, "Nursing and Patient Care," in *The Nursing Profession: Five Sociological Essays*, ed. Fred Davis (New York: John Wiley and Sons, 1966), 187-188; Brown, *Nursing for the Future*, 72.
5. Eleanor C. Lambertsen, *Nursing Team Organization and Functioning* (New York: Teachers College Press, Columbia University, 1953), 18.
6. David Wagner, "The Proletarianization of Nursing in the United States, 1932-1946," *International Journal of Health Services* 10(2) (1980): 271-290.
7. Ginzberg, *Program for the Nursing Profession*, 39-40.
8. Brown, *Nursing for the Future*, 75. Also, see Ginzberg, *Program for the Nursing Profession*, 35.
9. For discussions of the above points see Brown, *Nursing for the Future*, chap. 3, 5, and 6; Ginzberg, *Program for the Nursing Profession*, chap. 3, 4, and 7.
10. For discussions of the team approach, see Ginzberg, *Program for the Nursing Profession*, chap. 3 and 5; Brown, *Nursing for the Future*, chap. 3.
11. Ginzberg, *Program for the Nursing Profession*, 38.
12. Ibid., 40.
13. Brown, *Nursing for the Future*, chap. 3.
14. Kathleen Cannings and William Lazonick, "The Development of the Nursing Labor Force in the United States: A Basic Analysis," in *Organization of Health Workers and Labor Conflict*, ed. Samuel Wolfe (Amityville, N.Y.: Baywood, 1978), 99.

15. Ibid., 97-103.
16. Lambertsen, *Nursing Team Organization*. For full citation, see n. 5.
17. For further discussion of RNs' responsibilities, see Lambertsen, *Nursing Team Organization*, chap. 3, 4, and 7.
18. Dorothy Deming, *The Practical Nurse* (New York: The Commonwealth Fund, 1947), 70-71.
19. Lambertsen, *Nursing Team Organization*, 16-17, 47.
20. Ibid., 12.
21. See, for example, the bibliographies in Frances L. George and Ruth P. Kuehn, *Patterns of Patient Care* (New York: MacMillan, 1955); Ethel A. Brooks, "Team Nursing—1961," *American Journal of Nursing* (Apr. 1961): 87-91.
22. Cannings and Lazonick, "Development of the Nursing Labor Force," table 7.
23. Robert W. Habenstein and Edwin A. Christ, *Professionalizer, Traditionalizer, and Utilizer* (Columbia: University of Missouri Press, 1955); Leonard Reissman and John H. Rohrer, eds., *Change and Dilemma in the Nursing Profession* (New York: G. P. Putnam's Sons, 1957). For a complete bibliography of studies sponsored by the American Nurses' Association, see Everett Hughes, Helen MacGill Hughes, and Irwin Deutscher, *Twenty Thousand Nurses Tell Their Story: A Report on Studies of Nursing Functions Sponsored by the American Nurses' Association* (Philadelphia: J. B. Lippincott, 1958).
24. Hughes, Hughes, and Deutscher, *Twenty Thousand Nurses*, 82, 131, 135. Full citation noted above.
25. Hughes' perspective on professionalization guided his interpretation of empirical studies of nursing and is contained in numerous essays. See Everett C. Hughes, *The Sociological Eye: Selected Papers* (Chicago: Aldine-Atherton, 1971); also, see an earlier volume entitled *Men and Their Work* (New York: Free Press, 1958).
26. Hughes, *Sociological Eye*, 314.
27. Reissman and Rohrer, "The Changing Role of the Professional Nurse," in *Change and Dilemma in the Nursing Profession*, 10.
28. For a theoretical discussion of occupational and work jurisdictions, see Andrew Abbott, *The System of Professions* (Chicago: University of Chicago Press, 1988). With respect to health care, see Eliot Freidson, *Profession of Medicine* (New York: Dodd, Mead, 1970; Chicago: University of Chicago Press, 1988), chap. 3; also, Freidson, "Paramedical Personnel," in *International Encyclopedia of the Social Sciences*, ed. David L. Sills (New York: MacMillan and The Free Press, 1968), 10: 114-120.
29. Hughes, *Sociological Eye*, 298-301, 338-347.
30. Hughes, Hughes, and Deutscher, *Twenty Thousand Nurses*, 136-140.
31. Ibid., 174.
32. Ibid., 146, 174-175.

33. Ibid., 230-231.

34. Ibid., 228.

35. See Hughes, *Sociological Eye*, Part 3.

36. Hughes, Hughes, and Deutscher, *Twenty Thousand Nurses*, 150.

37. Hughes acknowledged in his early essays that his work was more focused on "the social psychological, rather than with the organizational aspects of work; and with the professional and would-be professional rather than with the industrial and bureaucratic occupations." Hughes, *Men and Their Work*, 8.

38. Eliot Freidson, *Professional Dominance* (New York: Atherton, 1970), 128, 132.

39. Freidson, *Profession of Medicine*, 69.

40. Ibid., 65.

41. On the development of hospitals and their bureaucratic features before the post-World War II period, see Charles E. Rosenberg, *The Care of Strangers* (New York: Basic Books, 1987). On the bureaucratic context of nursing practice in postwar hospitals, see Hans O. Mauksch, "The Organizational Context of Nursing Practice," in *The Nursing Profession*, ed. Fred Davis (New York: John Wiley and Sons, 1966), 109-137. For the distinction between autonomous and heteronomous professional organizations, see W. Richard Scott, "Reactions to Supervisors in a Heteronomous Professional Organization," *Administrative Science Quarterly* 10(1) (1965): 65-81. Scott's initial study was conducted among social workers. For his discussion of health care occupations, see "Managing Professional Work: Three Models of Control for Health Organizations," *Health Services Research* 17(3) (Fall 1982): 213-239. The semiprofessional status of nursing is discussed in Amitai Etzioni, ed., *The Semi-Professions and Their Organization: Teachers, Nurses, Social Workers* (New York: Free Press, 1969).

42. For a discussion of the importance of making this distinction, see Harry Braverman, *Labor and Monopoly Capital* (New York: Monthly Review Press, 1974), chap. 3.

43. George and Kuehn, *Patterns of Patient Care*. For additional comments about Lillian Gilbreth's role in the rationalization of nursing tasks, see Susan Reverby, "The Search for the Hospital Yardstick: Nursing and the Rationalization of Hospital Work," in *Health Care in America: Essays in Social History*, ed. Susan Reverby and David Rosner (Philadelphia: Temple University Press, 1979), 206-225; also Susan M. Reverby, *Ordered to Care* (Cambridge: Cambridge University Press, 1987), chap. 8. Scientific management was also used to rationalize work in support departments as hospital service workers were introduced on a larger scale throughout the 1940s and 1950s. See Robert E. Smalley and John R. Freeman, *Hospital Industrial Engineering: A Guide to the Improvement of Hospital Management Systems* (New York: Reinhold Publishing Corporation, 1966).

44. For a larger discussion of the literature on the proletarianization of professional occupations that includes the distinction between workers' loss of control over the means of labor ("technical proletarianization") and a loss of control over the product or ends of labor ("ideological proletarianization"), see Charles Derber, "Toward a New Theory of Professionals as Workers: Advanced Capitalism and Postindustrial Labor," in *Professionals as Workers*, ed. Charles Derber (Boston: G. K. Hall, 1982), 193-208. For a discussion of the deskilling of white-collar labor, including service and semiprofessional occupations, see Braverman, *Labor and Monopoly Capital*, chap. 15, 16, 18. On nursing, see Wagner, "The Proletarianization of Nursing," 271-290. I mentioned Wagner's thesis in my discussion of private duty nursing in chap. 3. For a related discussion on the possible proletarianization of medicine, see my discussion in chap. 2, which includes additional citations to the sociological debate on professional decline.

45. See earlier discussion of Hughes' interpretation of team nursing and text quotation corresponding with n. 24.

46. Reverby, "Search for the Hospital Yardstick," 217.

47. Barbara Melosh also acknowledges that RNs' tasks were upgraded with hospital employment during the team nursing period. *The Physician's Hand: Work Culture and Conflict in American Nursing* (Philadelphia: Temple University Press, 1982), 184.

48. See Braverman, *Labor and Monopoly Capital* for a discussion of the managerial advantages of subdividing labor.

49. For discussions of delegated responsibility and autonomy in a variety of occupations and work settings, including industrial manufacturing, see Andrew L. Friedman, *Industry and Labour* (London: MacMillan, 1977); Alan Fox, *Beyond Contract: Work, Power, and Trust Relations* (London: Faber and Faber, 1974); Andrew Herman, "Conceptualizing Control: Domination and Hegemony in the Capitalist Labor Process," *The Insurgent Sociologist* 11(3) (Fall 1982): 7-22; Michael Burawoy, *Manufacturing Consent: Changes in the Labor Process under Monopoly Capitalism* (Chicago: University of Chicago Press, 1979).

50. See my discussion of primary nursing in chap. 5.

51. As I have pointed out, unlike Wagner, Melosh argues that nurses were not deskilled. Nevertheless, their arguments are similar inasmuch as both argue that the integrity of the occupation's work was destroyed by the subdivision of tasks. See Melosh, *Physician's Hand*, 204; Wagner, "Proletarianization of Nursing."

52. On social relations between RNs and auxiliaries, see Hughes, Hughes, and Deutscher, *Twenty Thousand Nurses*, chap. 7; Temple Burling, Edith M. Lentz, and Robert N. Wilson, *The Give and Take in Hospitals* (New York: G. P. Putnam's Sons, 1956), chap. 11. Such views of subordinate workers are not uncommon. See Fox, *Beyond Contract*.

53. Habenstein and Christ, *Professionalizer, Traditionalizer, and Utilizer*, 80.

54. Similarly, practical nurses and aides told researchers in the 1950s that they resented being "on the receiving end of orders all of the time." Burling, Lentz, and Wilson, *Give and Take in Hospitals*, 155.

55. Bureaucratic rules and formal job descriptions were widely implemented in hospitals throughout the 1950s to stabilize relations among RNs and auxiliaries. Burling, Lentz, and Wilson interviewed a nursing administrator who was instituting detailed job descriptions "to increase the feeling of stability and security in her workers." *Give and Take in Hospitals*, 149. For a larger discussion of the managerial benefits of bureaucratic control, see Richard Edwards, *Contested Terrain* (New York: Basic Books, 1979), chap. 8.

56. Hughes discussed similar features of overlapping tasks. See Hughes, Hughes, and Deutscher, *Twenty Thousand Nurses*, 131-150.

57. For a discussion of the assimilation of professional knowledge by subordinate workers in professional hierarchies, see Abbott, *System of Professions*, 64-69.

58. Theodore Caplow, *The Sociology of Work* (New York: McGraw-Hill, 1954), 246.

59. Margaret Levi, "Functional Redundancy and the Process of Professionalization: The Case of Registered Nurses in the United States," *Journal of Health Politics, Policy and Law* 5(2) (Summer 1980): 333-353.

60. For an insightful discussion of the 1974 RN strike in San Francisco, see David Gaynor et al., "RN's Strike: Between the Lines," in *Prognosis Negative*, ed. David Kotelchuck (New York: Vintage, 1976), 229-245.

61. Burling, Lentz, and Wilson, *Give and Take in Hospitals*, 153.

62. Quoted in Virginia H. Walker, "The Informal Structure and Functioning of the Premature Center," in *Change and Dilemma in the Nursing Profession*, ed. Reissman and Rohrer, 207.

63. Leonard Reissman, "Social Psychological Characteristics of the Hospital Employee," in *Change and Dilemma in the Nursing Profession*, ed. Reissman and Rohrer, 154.

64. Edwin A. Christ, *Nurses at Work* (Columbia: University of Missouri Press, 1956), 60. Quoted in Hughes, Hughes, and Deutscher, *Twenty Thousand Nurses*, 149.

65. Hughes, Hughes, and Deutscher, *Twenty Thousand Nurses*, 179.

66. Ibid., 178-179.

67. For a general discussion of the sources of empowerment among subordinate workers, see David Mechanic, "Sources of Power of Lower Participants in Complex Organizations," *Administrative Science Quarterly* 7(3) (1962): 349-364.

68. The effects of race were complex and may have varied by region. In southern hospitals, race may actually have contributed to the *acceptance* of nurses' aides. Hughes summarized the relationship in the following remarks.

> In the premature center in New Orleans, where the professional staff disapproved of practical nurses, attendants were thought of as reliable and desirable: "our attendants know their place." The attendants are Negroes, and they simply carry into the hospital the position that they hold in the Southern caste system. They are much less likely to "overstep" than white attendants might be.

Hughes, Hughes, and Deutscher, *Twenty Thousand Nurses*, 175. For the original documentation of this case, see Walker, "Informal Structure and Functioning," in *Change and Dilemma in the Nursing Profession*, ed. Reissman and Rohrer, 207-208.

69. Hughes, Hughes, and Deutscher, *Twenty Thousand Nurses*, 236; Habenstein and Christ, *Professionalizer, Traditionalizer, and Utilizer*.

70. Burling, Lentz, and Wilson, *Give and Take in Hospitals*, 154-155.

71. Leonard Reissman, "The Hospital Structure," in *Change and Dilemma in the Nursing Profession*, ed. Reissman and Rohrer, 107.

72. As I argued earlier in the chapter, functional nursing existed as a formal model that was modified and combined with other forms of work organization, including the team approach.

CHAPTER 5

Reunified Tasks: Primary Nursing and the Trend to an All-RN Work Force

In this chapter I discuss the reorganization of nursing and the development of RN-predominant forms of practice during the cost containment era of the 1970s and 1980s. "Primary nursing" provided the leading model and ideology of professionalization, although in practice it included a variety of adaptations to organizational and staffing constraints, including the continued presence of some auxiliaries. I employ the term to characterize a generic form of labor that reunified nursing tasks and returned RNs to the bedside. However, I critique nursing leaders' argument that reunified tasks and an unmediated relationship between the RN and the patient constitute the essence of professional practice. Although primary nursing originated as an elite occupational strategy for professional upgrading, like team nursing, it resulted from the convergence of potentially disparate interests.

My detailed case study of primary nursing at Pacific Hospital reveals why RNs cooperated in its implementation, and the subsequent costs to them. Primary nursing constituted a subordinate but reorganized work process that overcame the problems of team nursing yet intensified RNs' labor, serving managerial interests and forcing RNs to devise strategies to deal with the burden of an overextended work jurisdiction. Despite nursing leaders' claim that primary nursing would elevate RNs to a professional status comparable to that of physicians, in actuality, the reunification of tasks and the flattening of the nursing hierarchy not only intensified RNs' work, it increased their accountability to physicians and administrators. Dissatisfaction eventually undermined consent, resulting in an RN strike in 1987 which revealed that primary nursing not only had contradictory effects on RNs' work but on the empowerment of workers as well.

PRIMARY NURSING AS PROFESSIONALIZATION

Primary nursing originated in the late 1960s among nursing educators and administrators dissatisfied with the large number of auxiliary nurses on hospital wards and the failure of nursing to attain professional status. Nursing leaders advocated an organization of practice in which RNs would no longer supervise teams of auxiliaries but replace them at the bedside. Primary nursing would establish what contemporary nursing leaders now considered the most important features of professional nursing: an unmediated relationship between the RN and the patient, complete responsibility for patient care through reunified work tasks, and occupational autonomy within the hospital [1].

Nursing leaders realized that in subdividing labor, team nursing was similar to task-oriented functional nursing. However, they failed to recognize that in actual practice functional nursing and scientific management principles had never been strictly adhered to. Nor were they inclined to acknowledge that team nursing, the most successful adaptation of these principles, had upgraded RNs' tasks and responsibilities. Rather, nursing leaders maintained that the application of scientific management principles and the differentiation of nursing tasks had destroyed the integrity of professional practice, deprofessionalizing the occupation [2].

In advocating the reorganization of work, nursing leaders claimed that primary nursing would establish RNs' professional practice based on principles that had existed in private duty nursing, when graduate nurses were supposedly autonomous professionals performing complete nursing care in a one-to-one relationship with their patients. With the implementation of primary nursing and "total patient care," the integrity of nursing work would be restored. Nursing leaders argued that reunifying RNs' tasks corresponded with job enrichment, work humanization, and professionalization. Responsibility for patient care would be clearly assigned to individual RNs, as primary nursing was "grounded on the staff nurse's acceptance of personal responsibility—on responsibility not being shared" [3]. Just as patients commonly refer to their physician as "my doctor," without auxiliaries at the bedside, patients would now identify only the RN as "my nurse." Furthermore, through the reorganization of work, the occupation would finally attain its long pursued goal of collegiality with physicians. Physicians would coordinate their medical care with the primary nurse, communicating with the RN regarding the overall treatment of patients and seeking the nurse's opinion. Professional practice would finally come to hospital wards [4].

Primary nursing and total patient care were implemented throughout the 1970s and 1980s, reorganizing nursing so that RNs eventually predominated on the wards and at the bedside. At the University of Minnesota Hospital where primary nursing is often said to have begun, nurses' aides were for the most part displaced to non-nursing activities in housekeeping, food service, and transportation [5]. LPNs were retained and assigned their own patients, an arrangement that contradicted the principle that only the professional nurse should be given responsibility for patients' complete care [6]. If primary nursing was to be successful, many nursing leaders believed that auxiliaries had to be entirely replaced. Consequently, primary nursing and the reunification of tasks became associated with a trend toward an all-RN work force in hospitals [7].

Although few hospitals completely replaced auxiliaries, the effect of primary nursing on the composition of workers and the organization of work was dramatic. As the first wave of hospitals implemented primary nursing, Luther Christman indicated that at Rush Presbyterian-St. Luke's Medical Center in Chicago between 1973 and 1977, the hospital's labor force was transformed from the conventional mode established under team nursing (approximately two-thirds auxiliaries and one-third RNs) to the opposite staffing mode of two-thirds RNs and one-third auxiliaries [8]. A similar process was occurring at other hospitals, and although these institutions were more likely to retain LPNs than nurses' aides, in many cases, staffing with both was gradually reduced [9].

The reorganization of work on hospital wards continued into the 1980s as institutions that lagged behind were eager to implement the change. By the mid-1980s, variations of primary nursing and the trend toward an all-RN work force had displaced team nursing at hospitals nationwide. As a result, RN staffing, as a percentage of *national* hospital nursing personnel, was now reversed from the pattern prevailing in the industry during the team nursing period. Whereas RNs comprised only 33 percent of all hospital nursing personnel in the late

1960s and auxiliaries 67 percent, by the late 1980s, only twenty years later, RNs had increased to 63 percent and auxiliaries' presence on hospital wards had declined to 37 percent (Table 1).

Throughout this reorganization period, nursing educators and administrators were forced to adapt primary nursing to the realities of hospital wards and to the continued presence of some auxiliary nurses. Initially, nursing educators emphasized that the primary nurse would retain responsibility for patients' care twenty-four hours a day throughout each patient's hospitalization. However, maintaining such a level of continuity was difficult. It was impractical for the primary nurse's responsibility to extend to a patient's complete hospitalization because patients are often transferred from one ward to another during the course of their illness. Although patient transfers do not pose a problem for physicians, whose relationship with patients is autonomous of hospital administration, nurses are assigned to particular wards. When patients are moved, responsibility for nursing care is assumed by a different nurse [10]. Even when a patient remains on the same ward throughout their hospitalization, RNs generally do not welcome a level of responsibility that could conceivably extend to phone calls at home when off duty, visits to the hospital during emergencies as is typical for physicians, and inflexibility in changing patient

Table 1. Changes in the Composition of Hospital Nursing Personnel, Selected Years

| Year | Total Personnel | Percent of Total | | | |
		Prof. RNs	Nonprof. Combined	LPNs	NAs
1968	956,053	33	67	19	48[a]
1979	1,361,424	46	54	19	35
1988	1,406,036[b]	63	37	16	21

Note: Prof. = professional; Nonprof. = nonprofessional; RNs = registered nurses; LPNs = licensed practical nurses; NAs = nurses' aides.

[a]Exact percentage of NAs reported for 1968 is slightly inconsistent.

[b]Total personnel for 1988 is from unpublished data, American Hospital Association, Annual Survey of Hospitals.

Sources: Linda H. Aiken, Robert J. Blendon, and David E. Rogers, "The Shortage of Hospital Nurses: A New Perspective," *American Journal of Nursing* (Sept. 1981), 1616; American Hospital Association, *Hospital Nursing in the '90s* (Chicago: American Hospital Association, 1991), 26-27.

assignments. In addition, not only does part-time employment, common for many RNs, mitigate against continuous responsibility, but nurses work only one shift during a twenty-four hour period [11]. Although primary nurses were formally accountable for each patient's care, in practice an "associate" nurse took care of the patient when the primary nurse was off duty. To maintain responsibility, the primary nurse was supposed to write detailed "nursing orders" in nursing care plans, so that the associate nurse could follow the primary nurse's directions [12].

Further complications arose when the associate nurse was an LPN or nurse's aide. Some hospitals allowed auxiliaries to work as primary nurses, but this suggested either that LPNs and nurses' aides could function adequately in the professional role or that some patients did not need the care of a professional nurse. Remaining auxiliaries, therefore, were often restricted to the associate role of caring for patients when the primary nurse was off duty. However, even restricting auxiliaries to this secondary role maintained an internal nursing hierarchy that was likely to raise some of the same problems that existed in team nursing. It was easier to formally differentiate the auxiliaries' role than it was in practice to control their work.

Because of such incongruities, prior to an RN shortage in the late 1980s, many nursing educators continued to advocate an all-RN work force. If primary nursing was to fulfill its claim to professional practice, RNs would have to assume full responsibility for the complete care of all patients [13]. Professional nurses could then relate as colleagues in the same way physicians do when they cover for one another when off duty. However, with the onset of the RN shortage, the trend toward an all-RN work force slowed. In some cases auxiliaries were reintroduced, although in much fewer numbers than had existed in team nursing [14]. RN staffing still prevailed on the wards, but the presence of auxiliaries, even at reduced levels, continued to generate debate as to the role of nonprofessional nurses in primary nursing and whether their presence nullified the claim to professional practice [15].

For all the reasons I have mentioned and no doubt other reasons as well, primary nursing was adapted to organizational constraints, creating considerable variation in actual practice on hospital wards. Although nursing educators have often viewed deviations from the ideal as undesirable, adaptation was critical to the displacement of team nursing. Moreover, a dramatic increase in RN staffing and the assignment of patients' total care (reunified tasks) to individual nurses is common to primary nursing regardless of variation, and is the basis of claims to professional upgrading. Thus, although the term "primary nursing" may be losing cachet in the nursing literature in the 1990s, as a form of labor with considerable variation to accommodate organizational and staffing constraints, it transformed the organization of nursing on hospital wards in the 1970s and 1980s and still exists in the terms I have defined.

THE LIMITS OF PROFESSIONALIZATION

Despite its success in displacing team nursing, the professional claims for primary nursing and the reality on hospital wards have not been critically examined. As we have seen, contemporary nursing leaders claimed that team nursing had deprofessionalized the occupation and that primary nursing incorporated professional principles exemplified in private duty before RNs' employment in hospitals. In making this argument, nursing leaders ignored the realities of both team nursing and private duty nursing. As I discussed in Chapter 3, private duty nurses were subject to intense market competition with practical nurses who also had a direct relationship with patients and performed their complete nursing care, yet were certainly not considered professional nurses. Furthermore, graduate nurses' access to employment was controlled by hospital registries and physicians, and their employment by private households created working conditions that inhibited the development of professional autonomy. Not surprisingly, RNs were greatly dissatisfied with private duty, and this type of work remains a less esteemed branch of nursing today.

In arguing that primary nursing is more professional than team nursing, contemporary nursing leaders have disregarded sociological theories of professionalization as well as claims by their predecessors that *team nursing* professionalized the occupation. Theories of professionalization do not support the assertion that reunified tasks and an unmediated relationship with clients constitute professional principles of practice. In fact, as I discussed in Chapter 4, team nursing exemplified sociological theories of professionalization more closely than does primary nursing. The shedding of routine tasks remains one of the critical features of professional upgrading. Thus, Andrew Abbott points out that the inclusion of routine tasks within an occupational jurisdiction seriously compromises the ability of an occupation to upgrade its work [16]. To claim that the professionalization of nursing requires RNs resume tasks formerly delegated to auxiliary workers reverses the differentiation of tasks characteristic of professionalization.

The creation of an unmediated relationship between RNs and patients is also a questionable criteria for professional upgrading. Abbott has argued that professional status is typically advanced through "professional regression," that is to say, by moving away from direct and routine client involvement. The occupational segment most involved with the occupation's knowledge base generally has the highest professional status [17]. Despite the claim that primary nursing upgrades the occupation by establishing an unmediated relationship with patients, the most professionalized segments of nursing continue to pursue advanced credentialing and typically leave patient care for careers in education or administration.

Furthermore, the labor force that made the conversion to primary nursing possible lacked a level of credentialing that would sustain a collective claim to professional status. Although the ANA has advocated the baccalaureate degree as the professional credential since 1965, nursing has remained class-stratified, and throughout the 1970s and 1980s the majority of staff nurses continued to lack this credential. With the decline of hospital training schools, the education of RNs did shift from hospitals to collegiate settings. However, community college programs prevailed over baccalaureate programs, and RNs with two year associate degrees provided the major supply of primary nurses [18]. Community colleges are more likely to be attended by students from working class rather than middle class backgrounds, and the credentials acquired are intended for technical rather than professional occupations. Since the majority of primary nurses lacked more advanced degrees, it would appear that a higher level of credentialing is not necessary for adequate performance as a primary nurse. In fact, RNs with community college, hospital diploma, and university degrees have all qualified for licensure and worked as primary nurses, demonstrating a weak linkage between educational credentialing and the reality of work on hospital wards [19].

A REORGANIZED LABOR PROCESS

As we have seen, nursing leaders' claim that primary nursing professionalizes the occupation is tenuous. I will argue that primary nursing, like team nursing, is a subordinate labor process created through a convergence of professional and managerial interests. Although primary nursing originated as an elite occupational strategy for professionalization, the implementation of primary nursing and the trend toward an all-RN work force would have failed if it had served only occupational interests. Primary nursing displaced team nursing during the cost containment era of the 1970s and 1980s, when rising health care expenditures forced non-health care corporations and the state to pressure hospitals to contain costs. As discussed in Chapter 2, hospitals responded by reorganizing into diversified health care corporations at the same time that they attempted to hold labor costs down and increase productivity.

The widespread implementation of primary nursing rested on convincing hospital administrators of the economic and managerial advantages to be gained. A proliferation of studies by nursing educators claimed that primary nursing increased RNs' work satisfaction, reduced labor turnover and absenteeism, and improved the quality of patient care. As the pressures of cost containment mounted, nursing studies emphasized that primary nursing was more economical than team nursing and was therefore compatible with state and corporate cost control programs [20].

The replacement of auxiliaries with RNs can seem puzzling as the reunification of tasks contradicts scientific management and the Babbage principle that subdividing tasks and employing cheaper labor to perform routine tasks is the most efficient means of organizing work. However, as political economists have pointed out, subdividing work does not automatically result in lower labor costs. Productivity has to be considered along with the wage differential among workers [21]. Hospital administrators were receptive to reversing the subdivision of labor when they discovered that doing so could increase labor productivity. Under the pressures of cost control and a greater emphasis on profitability, the reorganization of nursing work was based on managements' belief that RNs could be more productive than a stratified labor force that included auxiliary nurses. RNs' hourly wage was of course higher than that of auxiliaries, but as Aiken has shown, the differential overall was relatively narrow, and moreover, RNs could perform a wider range of nursing and nursing-related tasks without supervision. As a result, throughout the 1970s and most of the 1980s, management replaced auxiliaries with RNs, contributing to the recent shortage of RNs in the late 1980s [22].

Just as managerial and professional interests had converged in the 1950s to subdivide the labor process, these potentially disparate interests converged again in the 1970s and 1980s to reunify nursing tasks. But what of the interests of workers themselves? Why did RNs cooperate in the implementation of primary nursing and the displacement of auxiliaries, when the reunification of tasks was likely to intensify their labor? We lack sociological analyses of primary nursing that address this question. The literature is almost exclusively written by nursing educators whose goal has been to promote primary nursing and the professionalization of the occupation. It may be argued that staff nurses shared the optimism of nursing leaders and believed they would upgrade their work, or as some critics of professionalization have suggested, that RNs were deluded by a false consciousness, having internalized a professional ideology promulgated by elite groups [23].

In the case study that follows I examine the organization of nursing work at Pacific Hospital in the 1980s. Although nursing leaders and administrators did appeal to RNs' desire for professional status, I argue that primary nursing was not simply imposed, nor were RNs duped by professional ideology. To the extent that staff nurses possessed a professional consciousness, it derived principally from their sense of responsibility for patients, not from the attainment of professional status. To understand why RNs cooperated in the conversion to primary nursing and the displacement of auxiliaries, it is necessary to appreciate how the reorganization of work overcame the difficulties of team nursing. I then examine how that same transformation created new contradictions and failed to professionalize RNs' work.

A CASE STUDY:
PRIMARY NURSING AT PACIFIC HOSPITAL

Pacific Hospital had a national reputation for the quality of its nursing care, having received awards for its professional nursing practice with a high proportion of RNs. The hospital began implementing primary nursing in the early 1970s, and by the mid-1980s the work force consisted of approximately 85 percent RNs and 15 percent auxiliaries. Pacific Hospital continued to employ a few LPNs on each ward, but they were more likely to work on the evening or night shift rather than the day shift. By this time nurses' aides have been displaced, and before the RN shortage of the late 1980s, RNs believed that LPNs would eventually be replaced as well. Meanwhile, remaining LPNs were assigned their own patients and did not complete with RNs [24].

With the expansion of collegiate credentialing programs, RNs themselves were now more formally stratified. However, differential credentialing did not translate into clear status distinctions. Following the national pattern, most Pacific RNs had associate or hospital diploma degrees [25]. Only a minority had baccalaureate degrees, and they typically had attended a state college rather than a research university. Staff nurses commonly believed that university-educated RNs left nursing on the wards to pursue careers as administrators, teachers, or nurse practitioners. Regardless of the level of credentialing, all staff RNs were licensed to engage in the same work and did so. I could not discern skill distinctions among them, and presumably management could not either, as the job description for RNs had the same requirements for all. Furthermore, status distinctions among RNs were minimal [26]. I was unable to detect any relationship between degree level and one's reputation as a nurse. Typically RNs did not know who had what type of degree, and in many cases even shift charge nurses had diploma or associate degrees. "Good nurses" were nurses who could do the job well under pressure.

RNs had contradictory views about their standing in the occupational world. They took pride in their work and many complained that RNs were not given the recognition they deserve. However, the shift to primary nursing with a high proportion of RNs did not create a work culture in which most RNs believed they had been elevated to professional positions. Staff RNs rarely discussed issues debated in elite circles of the occupation, and when I asked about professionalism, I received mixed responses. Many felt that practicing RNs were members of a profession but often added that "doctors and administrators do not treat us like professionals." Others felt that RNs were "not professionals in the same way that doctors are." One associate degree RN who was considered an excellent nurse told me that "RNs who have left ward nursing talk more about professionalism. On the floors, it's still being able to do the job that counts." I was reminded of Fred Katz's comment twenty years earlier that "rank-and-file nurses generally appear to have less commitment to *professionalism* than their leaders" [27]. Yet, this same RN also stated that "there's something about being responsible for patients that we think of as being professional."

Similar comments by other RNs convinced me that nurses' sense of professionalism did not derive from having achieved professional status. As Freidson once argued, professionalism can exist as a set of attitudes apart from the attainment of that status. In this sense professionalism may also be considered a "false consciousness" that contributes to stability in the occupational hierarchy and to RNs' failure to identify with nonprofessional hospital workers. Freidson suggests it derives chiefly from the position of paraprofessionals in an occupational division of labor dominated by the medical profession [28]. However, there is also a lateral relationship between nurses and patients and a real experience of responsibility that is not derivative of an ideology imposed from above, and it is this understanding of professionalism that resonated with staff nurses on hospital wards despite their particular level of credentialing or failure to attain fully professionalized positions in the medical hierarchy. As discussed earlier, in team nursing auxiliaries' proximity to patients produced a quasi-professional consciousness among LPNs and aides. Similarly, RNs' professional consciousness was rooted in their experience of responsibility for patient care rather than the attainment of professional position.

Based on my case study of the reorganization of the work process at Pacific Hospital, I argue that primary nursing initially appealed to RNs because the reunification of tasks and the creation of an unmediated relationship with patients facilitated RNs' exercise of responsibility and control over nursing work. However, primary nursing also served managerial interests by intensifying RNs' labor. As a result, to overcome the problems of an overextended work jurisdiction, RNs were forced to omit some tasks formerly performed by auxiliaries and to shift others onto patients and their families. At the same time RNs had to limit patients' participation so that it did not keep them from getting their work done. Furthermore, despite elite claims to professionalization, RNs remained in a subordinate work jurisdiction, wherein the flattening of the nursing hierarchy actually increased their accountability to physicians and managers. By 1987, RNs' dissatisfaction with the intensification of work and continued subordination resulted in a strike. Ironically, although primary nursing had intensified RNs' work and increased their accountability, it also empowered RNs by eliminating their vulnerability to substitution by auxiliaries. Unfortunately, this was at the expense of a larger workplace solidarity with nonprofessional workers also burdened by work intensification.

Overcoming the Difficulties of Team Nursing

RNs were ambivalent about their professional status, but they considered primary nursing to have definite advantages over team nursing. As discussed in Chapter 4, team nursing contained contradictions that created problems on nursing wards. Although RNs' tasks and responsibilities had been upgraded, the effort to subdivide the labor process divided workers as well, creating tension between RNs and auxiliaries. RNs considered auxiliaries either inferior or excessively ambitious, while auxiliaries resented RNs' supervisory authority and assignment to higher level tasks, believing that they were left with the dirty work. Nevertheless, the rationalization of the labor process largely failed. The exigencies of work on the wards required RNs to delegate unauthorized tasks as well as participate in routine work formally assigned to LPNs and nurses' aides. Moreover, RNs were vulnerable to substitution by auxiliaries. RNs were unable to monopolize a core set of technical tasks, and auxiliaries were able to assimilate a knowledge of how to perform procedures formally reserved for the professional nurse. Furthermore, auxiliaries' continuous presence at the bedside provided a countervailing basis for their empowerment and created a competing experience of responsibility. Even after team nursing had been displaced, RNs at Pacific Hospital recalled the problems vividly. "Before Pacific switched to primary nursing we had what was called team nursing. It was terrible. Some of my worst nursing experiences were with team nursing."

For RNs, the critical difference between team and primary nursing was not the prospect of professional mobility, but a reunification of tasks that facilitated their exercise of responsibility without the problems that existed when auxiliaries mediated between RNs and patients. RNs were no longer threatened by auxiliaries' ability to substitute and were no longer forced to delegate work or violate formal rules while doing so. Most importantly, RNs insisted that primary nursing was an advance over team nursing because they were no longer responsible for care produced by auxiliaries. RNs now had complete control over the work for which they were accountable. An RN summarized the advantages in the following comments:

> Team nursing was difficult because the LPNs and nurses' aides were at the bedside, but we had responsibility for the care they gave the patients. When we told them what to do, they resented it. We're still responsible for nursing care, but we're no longer responsible for auxiliaries' work.

Another contributed, "Yes, and our licenses are no longer on the line!" Although they could not remember when an RN had actually lost their license due to an auxiliary nurse's performance, RNs sometimes made such comments to express their frustration at being accountable for care produced by other workers.

Furthermore, although primary nursing eliminated RNs' supervisory position over auxiliary bedside workers, it maintained RNs' autonomy within the nursing hierarchy. RNs were no longer team leaders, but neither did they experience close supervision by head nurses or shift charge nurses. With corporatization and greater responsibility for cost containment, the head nurse's role became more removed from production. They were now referred to as "unit managers" and their time was taken up with the budget, utilization review, DRGs, coordination of policies with other departments, and meetings. In addition, although the shift charge nurse might be considered a first-line supervisor, the role was clearly distinct from the supervisory relationship team leaders had with auxiliaries. While the charge nurse worked at the nursing station to coordinate activities and to process doctors' orders, the primary nurse was the indispensable figure on the wards. Charge nurses were dependent upon the knowledge and skills of primary nurses, who planned, organized and performed "total patient care" for all their patients [29].

Intensified Work: Total Patient Care

Although primary nursing elicited RNs' cooperation in the reorganization of work by overcoming the difficulties of team nursing and facilitating RNs' exercise of responsibility and control, it also created new dilemmas. As primary nursing displaced auxiliaries and reunified tasks, the "professional" work jurisdiction was enlarged to encompass "total patient care," which included the routine tasks formerly delegated to auxiliaries as well as the conceptual and skilled tasks assigned to RNs. In other words, now RNs had to organize the work to be done and then perform it all.

RNs' conceptual work began in shift report, which consumed the first thirty to forty-five minutes of the shift and took place throughout the hospital at 7 a.m., 3 p.m., and 11 p.m. RNs' responsibility and autonomy were clearly evident in that neither doctors nor unit managers were present. During report, RNs followed a standard procedure with similar rituals from ward to ward. As the shift charge nurse or individual RNs going off duty gave an update on each patient's current status, oncoming RNs listened, took notes, and occasionally interrupted to ask questions or make comments when detailed information about their patients was communicated [30].

Although report was the most sedentary activity RNs engaged in during the shift and could seem uneventful compared to patient care out on the floor, the work done in report involved more than simply communicating and recording information. During report RNs passed on responsibility for their patients and actively engaged in planning how they would accomplish the complete range of nursing tasks for all of their patients. In organizing the work to be done, RNs created worksheets that by the end of the shift appeared soiled and crumpled. Yet the RNs' work, its documentation in patients' charts, and report to the oncoming nurse could not be accomplished without them. Nurses referred to their worksheets throughout the shift, and when one RN had misplaced her worksheet and was frantic to find it, she exclaimed: "I've lost my brains! Has anybody seen my brains?" The charge nurse, sensing my bewilderment, contributed: "Our brains are in our heads. She's talking about her worksheet." Still, the association of the worksheet with conceptualization was unmistakable.

RNs created their worksheets as report was given on their patients. After listing the patient's name, bed number, diagnosis, and doctor, the nurse listened for information about each patient's various body systems. She or he noted critical information about the patient's medical status and their nursing needs, including vital signs (pulse, respirations, temperature, blood pressure), breath sounds, oxygen setting, blood gases, abnormal lab values.[1] The nurse carefully considered cardiovascular data and the status of the patient's IV (composition and rate of intravenous fluids), as well as basic information about the patient's gastrointestinal and genitourinary functioning: fluid intake and output, catheters, and any problems with incontinence. She recorded problems with skin care, need for turning the patient in bed, and for ambulation, in addition to a variety of reminders or comments regarding lab specimens to be collected, special treatments to be performed, emotional and family problems, special medications, and so on. As nurses repeated this procedure for each patient, they frequently consulted the Kardex, a file that contained a detailed record of the physician's current medical orders, checking the medications due, the diet order, changes in treatments, therapies, and various other orders for the care of the patient. The Kardex also contained the nursing care plans that RNs were to keep current.

While processing information about their patients, RNs associated doctors' orders and patients' needs with nursing tasks, making a complex assessment of what had to be done during the shift. RNs no longer faced the problem of which tasks to delegate to LPNs and nurses' aides,

---

[1] The overwhelming majority of RNs were women. For a discussion of gender segregation in nursing, see Christine L. Williams, *Gender Differences at Work* (Berkeley: University of California Press, 1989).

but because RNs' work now encompassed a much larger jurisdiction, they had to pay particular attention to prioritizing their tasks. In doing so, each confronted similar questions:

> Which patients will take most of my time?
> How serious are their medical-nursing needs?
> In what order should I see my patients?
> What do I have to do for each patient?
> Which tasks have priority?
> How long will it take me?
> How can I coordinate all tasks for each patient; for all my patients?

As they organized their work, RNs tried to anticipate some of the problems they would encounter. As one nurse did so, she reminded herself that

> Mr. Thomas is going to surgery immediately after report, so I'll need to give pre-op meds. Afterwards I'll check all my patients, then I need to do the dressing change on Ms. Cline before she goes for her scan. The phlebotomist is late in drawing blood for the tests Dr. Jones ordered, and he's the doctor who gave Pat a hard time last week. Better check with the lab. And, I'm supposed to get the first admission!

Effectively organizing the work to be done was critical to meeting the demands of the work process [31]. In the words of an experienced RN,

> by the time you leave report you know how heavy your assignment is going to be. You know which patients have the greater needs. You've thought about what you have to do and how you're going to go about it. You know whether you have time to talk with your patients or whether it's just going to be getting the basic care done.

Throughout the shift RNs continually revised their conceptualization of the work to be done, mentally sorting and evaluating new information, including new medical orders and of course, patients' immediate needs. As nurses engaged in patient care, they documented information on their worksheets that they later recorded in patients' charts and reported to nurses on the next shift.

While the demands of reunified tasks were evident in the conceptual work required of each RN, the burden of primary nursing weighed more heavily once RNs engaged in labor on the floors. Rather than job enrichment, the reunification of tasks constituted job enlargement and an intensification of work. Without auxiliaries, RNs passed the meal trays and took routine vital signs on all patients at different times throughout the shift. RNs also performed the dirty work of helping patients use bedpans, urinals, and bedside commodes; changing patients' soiled gowns and bed linens; lifting and moving patients; cleaning patients up after vomiting, incontinence, and diarrhea; and giving baths. Sometimes patients needed to be turned frequently to prevent skin breakdown or respiratory complications. In addition to the routine and dirty work, RNs also performed more of the emotional work that had been previously performed by auxiliaries because of their greater presence at the bedside [32]. "Tender loving care" or "TLC," as it was called, included such tasks as listening and talking to patients, giving backrubs, or simply holding a patient's hand for reassurance. Although of low status medically, these services were important to patients, their personal comfort, and their hopes for recovery. RNs also absorbed many of the custodial tasks that resulted from patients' dependency during their hospitalization. They were asked to assist with phone calls, adjust the television set, turn lights on and off, open and close doors, and a variety of other tasks occasioned by the patient's confinement to a hospital bed.

Of course, RNs continued to perform the skilled tasks that had been assigned to them in team nursing. This included the administering of all medications, a demanding activity as patients were frequently on many medications that were given at different times, in different dosages, via different routes. "Giving meds" for five or six patients during an eight hour shift required attention to detail and organization so that errors were not made [33]. Some were given one time only, perhaps "ASAP" or "STAT" (now) while others were given "PRN" (as needed) or at regular intervals. RNs also started IVs, administered blood transfusions, performed dressing changes, nasogastric tube feedings, tracheal suctioning, bladder irrigations, blood transfusions, and assisted physicians with special procedures such as a lumbar puncture or a thoracentesis. And, when caught up with the demands of patient care, RNs still had to document that care in each patient's chart. The prestige of charting had disappeared along with the auxiliaries. It was a tiresome clerical task that frequently kept RNs from going home on time as they rushed at the end of shift to complete the required entries.

The intensification of RNs' work was made additionally difficult by changes in utilization and reimbursement for hospital services. After 1984, nurses felt keenly that patients' nursing needs or "acuity," as it was called, was rising. With changes in Medicare reimbursement and the implementation of diagnostically related groups (DRGs), patients were not as readily hospitalized and were more likely to be treated through outpatient services or at facilities providing lower levels of care. While this may have eliminated some unnecessary costs, RNs felt that when patients were hospitalized, they were more likely to be seriously ill. In addition, once admitted and treated, patients were frequently discharged earlier in the recuperative period of illness so that the cost of their care would fall under DRG reimbursement ceilings, creating a surplus for the hospital. Nurses believed that these patients sometimes had to be rehospitalized, and that they were likely to be in even worse condition, requiring more intense nursing care [34].

At the same time that auxiliary nurses were displaced and the demands of patient care were rising, management was attempting to reduce labor costs in support departments. These cutbacks contributed further to intensifying labor on the wards as nurses were dependent upon adequate services from a variety of paraprofessional and non-professional workers. Each day patients were transported to departments like radiology or physical therapy for the completion of tests and treatments ordered by physicians. And, even more frequently, diverse technical and support workers came to the wards to deliver food trays and supplies, to draw blood, or to perform portable X-rays, respiratory treatments, and a variety of other services. When supplies needed for patient care were slow coming to the wards, when meal trays were late, missing, or in error, or when housekeeping workers were unavailable to clean a room promptly, RNs produced care under more arduous conditions, sometimes performing the tasks themselves. In some cases, work was intentionally shifted onto nurses, as when RNs were required to perform heavy lifting and other tasks after management declared that an orderly was no longer needed on the evening shift [35].

Inadequate support service not only jeopardized timely task performance, it contributed to interdepartmental problems in managing patient care. Although they lacked formal authority over ancillary workers, RNs were responsible for coordinating these services with their nursing care. The RN might need the supply room clerk to bring an infusion pump to the floor before IV fluids could be started, food service to bring a snack for a diabetic patient, or the lab tech to draw a specimen for blood cultures before the RN started the IV antibiotics. As work was intensified both on the wards and in support departments, relations between RNs and peripheral department workers became more strained. Tension was often dispersed laterally among subordinate workers rather than toward managerial policies. Thus, when problems existed in the availability of support services, RNs typically complained about these workers, which only served to heighten the discord. Burawoy has noted similar processes of conflict dispersion in other work settings in which factory operatives were dependent upon ancillary services [36].

Nevertheless, RNs continued to prefer primary nursing over team nursing as reunified tasks and an unmediated relationship with patients gave them more control over nursing work. By overcoming the problems of team nursing, primary nursing elicited RNs' cooperation in what was effectively their own exploitation. However, RNs' comments also revealed their frustration with an overextended work jurisdiction. As one RN remarked:

> Sometimes when I am tired from running to keep up with the patients and the doctors, I think it was better for RNs when we were team leaders supervising auxiliary nurses. The trouble now is, they keep including more tasks and heavier assignments in which you have to do everything! I don't think we can take on much more.

Another RN with thirty years' experience recalled what she now viewed as the advantages of team nursing.

> Nurses used to have more authority and higher status in team nursing. We didn't have to do all this routine bedside care. You know, like emptying bedpans, changing beds, all the things that even a maid could do.

Still, RNs did not want to return to team nursing. Rather, they felt caught between the problems of team nursing and the costs of primary nursing. As one stated: "Primary nursing keeps you running and it's getting worse. We need some help but we don't want team nursing back." In some cases, RNs used the idiom of professionalism to convey the advantages of primary nursing, but on one occasion an RN revealed the contradiction as well: "Primary nursing is more professional, but RNs have to do more of the shit work."

Omitting Work, Shifting Work, and Controlling Patients' Participation

As we have seen, in reunifying tasks, primary nursing resolved the problems of team nursing at the same time that it intensified RNs' labor by enlarging their work jurisdiction to include the routine tasks formerly delegated to auxiliaries. Primary nursing also created a direct relationship with patients that fully exposed RNs to patients' needs and demands for services.

With reunified tasks and an unmediated relationship with patients, nursing care could require virtually the continuous presence of the RN at the bedside. Patients were oriented to their own individual medical problems and lacked an understanding of the pressures on RNs to perform complete care for five or six patients, a typical assignment on many medical wards. Earlier I discussed the wide range of patient care tasks that RNs now performed, including a heavy burden of routine tasks and dirty work as well as emotional, comfort, and non-nursing custodial tasks that resulted from patients' dependence. Nurses tried to accommodate patients as much as possible, however RNs were often overburdened and auxiliaries were no longer available to help.

RNs were frustrated by the incongruity between the ideology of primary nursing as professional upgrading and job enrichment, and the reality of work intensification and job enlargement. As professionals, RNs were supposed to be able to individually organize and perform complete nursing care for all their patients, but in daily life on the wards, RNs were faced with an overextended work jurisdiction. On one ward, RNs attempted to handle the problem by approaching nursing administration directly, suggesting that the hospital provide a written statement at the bedside explaining that because of staffing policies, RNs could no longer perform nonessential services that had been customary in the past and that patients might still expect. As one RN stated: "The hospital is not a luxury hotel. Management should take responsibility for informing patients that RNs no longer have the time to do personal service tasks that patients can do themselves." However, RNs soon learned that raising such issues with administrators was fruitless. To attract business, the hospital continued to promote its reputation for care by professional nurses, and RNs learned that complaints could affect their job evaluations adversely. RNs confided that when they talked to their unit manager about the additional burden of work on the wards they were told to improve their organizational skills, that "*professional* nurses should be able to get all their work done."

Because primary nursing individualized as well as intensified the work process, RNs also felt uncomfortable asking one another for assistance. This was not a problem if a task required more than one person or an RN needed the advice of a more experienced nurse. However, because RNs were overloaded with competing tasks, their efforts to complete their work within the shift could easily be disrupted. RNs were then forced to ask for help in situations in which it could appear that their organizational skills had failed. If RNs requested help too often under such circumstances, they could be perceived as unable to perform adequately. And if they asked for help without being available to reciprocate, they harmed relations with coworkers and were unlikely to receive cooperation in the future.

To get the essential work accomplished, RNs were forced to engage in strategies to limit their work load. Informally, RNs confided that nurses who attempted to consistently perform the complete range of services were likely candidates for "burnout," a term commonly used on the wards to refer to nurses' emotional exhaustion and loss of interest in truly caring about their patients. To ensure their completion of higher priority work within the time constraints of the shift, RNs attempted to limit their performance of lower-level tasks and to control what they now considered excessive patient demands for "luxury" services. A common strategy was simply to omit lower-level tasks when RNs found it necessary to do so. An RN with many years of experience stated that "patients got more personal care, more TLC under team nursing. They got more backrubs, baths, the personal care tasks, including more opportunities to talk with someone." Other RNs who had worked under both team and primary nursing agreed. "In team nursing auxiliaries were available to do this work. There are fewer nurses now, and we have to limit more of the personal service."

At the same time, restricting such work could be personally difficult, creating emotional work for nurses as they attempted to manage their own feelings about the care they provided. RNs usually felt an obligation to care for patients whether or not the tasks involved were associated with technical skills. As one RN put it, "nursing emphasizes the technical tasks, but what is important to the patient is TLC." Theoretically, the most mundane task was supposed to provide the opportunity to professionally assess patients and increase one's knowledge of their medical condition while also attending to the less tangible aspects of professional care, including the psycho-social needs of patients. However, it was often difficult to turn low-level tasks into professional tasks. As another RN confided, "How many times can you empty the bedpan and still convince yourself that this work contributes to your professional knowledge and practice?" In addition, unless intangible needs were defined as part of the medial diagnosis or were clearly hindering the patient's recovery, RNs were typically too busy to attend to them more than superficially.

Forced to engage in informal strategies to shrink their work juris-diction, RNs also attempted to shift tasks formerly performed by auxiliaries onto patients and their families. They did so by encouraging patients to take part in their own care. Of course, patient participation was needed in order for the nurse to produce care at all, as production and consumption were simultaneous. Patients contributed from the beginning of their hospitalization by providing information, donning a hospital gown, and cooperating in the production of services. However, with the displacement of auxiliaries, RNs informally redefined the boundary of production and consumption by encouraging patients to produce their own personal care at a level that RNs believed appro-priate to the patient's medical condition. Requests for RNs to perform simple tasks patients were capable of doing themselves were often considered unwarranted, and shifting this work onto patients was legitimized by an underlying view that it was therapeutic for patients to retain an active role in their care. Family members were also encouraged to participate by performing comfort tasks and emo-tional work that could consume a great deal of the RN's time. This was often considered not only appropriate but therapeutic for the family as well [37].

Shifting work onto patients and their families was tricky because it required RNs to renegotiate not only the boundaries of work but also the boundaries of patients' institutional dependence. On the one hand, the patient's dependence upon the nurse facilitated the RN's organiza-tion of the work to be done. On the other hand, the same dependency often led patients to demand services at a level that could overwhelm RNs' capacity to get everything accomplished before the work shift ended. RNs had to cleverly balance encouraging greater patient and family participation while remaining in control of core tasks and the overall organization of work. Stress could result not simply from the intensity of work but from the fear of losing control over it.

At the same time that patients were encouraged to perform self-care and family members to assist, there were definite limits on the level of participation that RNs appreciated. Questioning the nurse's priorities or attempting to participate in tasks that RNs considered clearly within their occupational jurisdiction was unwelcome. For the most part patients were limited in their capacity to interfere with nurses' core tasks as patients lacked knowledge of their illness, medical orders, and hospital procedures. Deviations were usually associated with the patient's or family's social status or a chronic patient's exceptional knowledge of their medical condition and hospital routines. However,

RNs commonly believed that patients and family members who were the most informed made nursing care more difficult because they tended to question the nurse excessively and to interfere with the management of nursing work. In one case a university professor negotiated with his family physician permission to administer most of his wife's medications. RNs cooperated, but offstage they complained that the arrangement made their work more complicated because they had trouble monitoring what medications the patient actually received. On the day the patient was to be discharged a medication error occurred, and the husband initiated complaints against the nursing staff. The case confirmed RNs' view that patient and family participation, while desirable, can jeopardize RNs' control of essential work and must be appropriately contained.

RNs limited patients' demands and controlled their participation by structuring the performance of work at the bedside. While patients were preoccupied with their own medical and nursing needs, RNs, in addition to being concerned about each patient, directed themselves to what had to be done for all patients within the time available. Primary nurses' understanding of the entire work load to be accomplished during the shift provided the context for assessing each patient's claims on their time and labor.

RNs structured the production of care at the bedside by making themselves readily available at certain times and relatively unavailable at other times, often negotiating such an understanding with patients. The process began immediately after shift report when RNs assessed their patients. Usually beginning with the patients to whom they intended to devote more time, RNs took vital signs and checked each patient's immediate medical condition and nursing needs. With patients who required less care, RNs quickly established parameters for patients' expectations, telling the patient that they would return when a medication was due, at which time they would be available to perform other tasks. The nurse reassured the patient that if they needed anything, they could use the call light. The ward clerk answered calls through an intercom at the nursing station and communicated the patient's request to the nurse. RNs often engaged the ward clerk's help in controlling the pace of work, cueing the clerk as to which calls should be immediately relayed, even when a nurse was busy in another patient's room, and which could be saved until the RN checked at the nursing station. Once the message was communicated, RNs had direct control over the response and its timing.

When patients did not acquiesce in the RN's structuring of their care, the nurse, with varying degrees of subtlety, attempted to educate patients to appropriate demands on his or her time and labor. Mutual agreements were made, with RNs frequently negotiating the timing of tasks and accommodating patients' preferences when the costs of doing so were not excessive. At other times, agreements had a more tacit character and were linked with different strategies RNs found effective for structuring their work. For example, one nurse used what she called a "saturation method" for handling patients who had a tendency to call too often with minor requests throughout the shift. When the nurse was in the patient's room performing a higher priority task, she asked the patient if they needed anything else and then followed through immediately on minor tasks while "saturating the patient with TLC" and suggesting that while it was alright to bring up minor requests at that time, she would not be pleased if the patient summoned her for tasks that could wait until she returned.

RNs viewed patients' requests as appropriate when their medical condition justified the concentration of the RN's time and energy, although they still complained sometimes about the difficulty of caring for such patients. With less support staff and sicker patients, nurses viewed patients who persistently demanded "nonessential" services as "problem patients," particularly if they interfered with RNs' performance of work that was considered to have higher priority. Lorber documented similar findings earlier, arguing that "ease of management was the basic criterion for a label of good patient, and that patients who took time and attention felt to be unwarranted by their illness tended to be labeled problem patients" [38]. The intensification of work on nursing wards in the 1970s and 1980s accentuated this tendency.

Occasionally there were patients who refused to cooperate, but a whole range of sanctions existed that led to compliance or an exit from the hospital. When efforts to educate patients failed, nurses sometimes ignored what they considered petty and repetitious demands. At times nurses' actions violated hospital rules so they had to be used judiciously, as when nurses intentionally delayed answering a patient's call light. In some situations, virtually the entire ward staff participated in strategies to give a beleaguered nurse a break and to quell the patient's demands. In handling difficult patients, nurses could move to more formal means of control by consulting with the charge nurse, who in talking with the patient might invoke hospital rules to elicit compliance or call the hospital's chief administrative nurse to the floor. If administrative authority failed, the nurse recorded the patient's lack of cooperation in the chart and notified the patient's physician. The patient who was unwilling to comply after a discussion with their doctor could sign out of the hospital "against medical advice," and a hospital form existed for this purpose. In one case a patient continued to be uncooperative but would not sign out, alienating both RNs and the physician. The physician then enlisted the help of nurses in having the patient transferred to the county psychiatric hospital. In another case, a patient simply removed his IV, got dressed, and walked out of the hospital.

These were extreme cases. Although patients did have the capacity to affect their care to the point of refusing it altogether, it is important not to overemphasize their prerogative. Patients were sick; they were vulnerable. They participated within the context of subordination to doctors' decisions and orders, hospital rules and procedures, and nurses' organization of their care. Patients had far more power over nurses in private duty nursing, when the role of the patient was combined with the role of employer. In the hospital, patients' ability to control nurses' labor is greatly reduced, while the power of nurses to structure and limit patients' demands is increased significantly [39]. With the intensification of work, RNs were forced to exercise their power to both enlist and limit patient participation. Yet they did so while they themselves remained subordinate to physicians and managers.

Continued Subordination to Physicians and Managers

I have argued that in displacing auxiliaries, reunifying tasks, and creating an unmediated relationship between the RN and the patient, primary nursing facilitated RNs' exercise of responsibility and control at the same time that it intensified their work, forcing them to engage in informal strategies to limit an overextended work jurisdiction. In the following discussion, I emphasize that this work jurisdiction remained subordinate to physicians, who continued to dominate the occupational hierarchy through their medical decisions, and also to managers, who maintained bureaucratic control. Furthermore, despite an ideology of professional upgrading, rather than attain colleagueship with physicians or challenge administrative control, the displacement of auxiliaries flattened the nursing hierarchy, reinforcing RNs' accountability.

Physicians' Professional Dominance

As I discussed in Chapter 2, physicians' power within the governing tripartite of Pacific Hospital was weakened somewhat by the corporate reorganization of the hospital and the growing power of management. However, physicians not only continued to participate in the governance of the institution, they continued to dominate the medical division of labor within it. Physicians were only on the hospital's wards for short periods of time, but they controlled the critical decisions of admitting and discharging patients, determining the medical diagnosis, and conceptualizing the overall plan of care that largely defined the labor of RNs and other workers. While RNs were at the top of the paramedical hierarchy, they did not decide on the critical medical problems to be addressed or the means of doing so. Their observation, discretion, and continuous presence on the hospital's wards were essential to meeting the medical objectives of physicians, but during the course of a patient's hospitalization, RNs were more likely to facilitate the production of care rather than define what that care should be.

Although both doctors and nurses talked of "admitting patients," only the doctor had the power to do so. In seeking medical help, the patient consulted a physician, not a nurse. The physician then decided whether to admit the patient to the hospital and communicated with the admitting department, which notified the appropriate ward of the admission. Only at that point was the patient assigned to the care of an RN.

The doctor's admitting diagnosis and plan for medical treatment determined the services produced by RNs and paraprofessional workers. Patients often arrived on the ward with admitting orders physicians wanted started immediately. These included orders for such things as routine blood tests, a urinalysis, chest X-ray or other diagnostic tests, an electrocardiogram and perhaps an order to start an intravenous medication. The nurse started the IV, collected the appropriate lab specimens, and ensured that other procedures were properly begun before the physician arrived. When patients arrived without admitting orders or came from the emergency room with minimal orders, the primary nurse performed the service of phoning the doctor for directives.

The nurse's admission of the patient was a secondary process that followed from the prior decisions of the physician. The RN assessed the patient's immediate medical condition and nursing needs while orienting the patient to their room. If the assessment indicated a need for prompt treatment, the RN called the patient's doctor to report the problem and to seek appropriate medical orders. On some occasions the nurse implemented physicians' standing orders for patients in distress (e.g., oxygen for patients suffering from severe shortness of breath). In emergency situations, the RN's actions were often critical to the well being of the patient and required the exercise of considerable skill and judgement. Nevertheless, these activities followed from the physician's decision to admit the patient and RNs' responsibility to the physician and the patient.

When the physician arrived on the ward, he or she examined the patient, checked any initial lab results, and wrote more comprehensive orders that specified much of the work the RN either performed or coordinated.[2] In formulating these directives the physician conceptualized what Strauss refers to as the "illness trajectory" and "the arc of work." Whereas RNs and paraprofessional workers had secondary spheres of responsibility, the physician was responsible "for ordering, evaluating and acting on diagnostic tests; for laying out the lines of work that need to be done; for utilizing the ward's organizational machinery" [40]. Physicians did so by writing detailed medical orders, including orders for all medications, diagnostic tests of the body's functioning and condition (X-rays, scans, EKGs), lab tests of body specimens, therapies (physical, respiratory), various nursing treatments (surgical/wound dressing changes), procedures for the care of the body's systems of elimination, intake and output measurements of fluids, skin care, frequency of vital signs, and even whether the patient could engage in such simple activities as get out of bed, drink fluids or eat. Physicians' orders also determined whether the patient would be seen by a medical specialist, receive the services of a variety of paraprofessionals, or be set up for surgery or for any special bedside procedures in which RNs assisted. Doctors indicated the priority they expected the RN and other workers to give to executing orders by specifying "ROUTINE," "ASAP" or "STAT" beside each order and using an indicator on the chart to flag the priority to be given to the entire set of orders.

---

[2] Although womens' participation in medicine is increasing, the vast majority of doctors were men. For a study of women in medicine, see Judith Lorber, *Women Physicians: Careers, Status, and Power* (New York: Tavistock, 1984).

A summary of the physician's orders, along with a nursing care plan generated by the primary nurse, were placed in a Kardex file for easy reference. The nursing care plan was to include a nursing diagnosis and nursing orders to be carried out by other RNs when the primary nurse was off duty and was advocated by the occupation's elite as part of their effort to establish RNs' professional expertise as comparable to that of physicians. Although new nurses had spent hours in school identifying nursing diagnoses and formulating care plans as part of their training, on the wards written care plans were not very important to the actual production of care, and new RNs quickly learned that these innovations were not taken seriously [41]. Care plans were rarely consulted and were often incomplete anyway as RNs considered writing detailed care plans a low priority and even a waste of time. With the intensity of the work, RNs resented being made to write down what they were supposed to do before actually doing it and then documenting their actions in the patient's chart [42]. In practice, RNs trusted each other's basic nursing knowledge and maintained continuity of care through shift report and informal personal interaction.

While the physician left the ward to see other patients in the hospital or return to his office practice, the RN proceeded to carry out the medical orders, which constituted an itemized list of the product to be produced. As I have indicated, the physician's orders specified many of the primary nurse's work activities. Some tasks were not specified by medical orders but derived from the RN's responsibility for work that, although important to the patient, was relegated to a secondary status by the physician. This included tasks involving body functions considered dirty work as well as many of the routine and custodial tasks I discussed earlier. The RN also informally assumed responsibility for coordinating and integrating diverse services ordered by the physician and produced by workers at lower levels in the hospital's division of labor.

Each day doctors visited the ward and briefly examined their patients. They checked the patient's chart for laboratory results and for technical information documented by the nurse: e.g., vital signs, input and output measurements, blood sugar results. They changed or wrote new orders if necessary, and before leaving the ward they usually noted the patient's condition in the "doctors' progress notes," which followed doctors' order sheets in the front of the patient's chart. RNs and paraprofessional workers documented their care on hospital forms in sections behind the doctors', reflecting the occupational division of labor and the hierarchy of professional responsibility.

Although nurses carried out the doctor's orders and continued to coordinate patients' care, they acted not simply as physicians' "hands," but also as physicians' eyes, ears, and brains, in the sense that they observed changes in patients' conditions, reported symptoms, sometimes suggested what was needed, and interpreted the effects of medical treatment. Because of RNs' continuous presence on the wards, doctors were dependent upon RNs for keeping them informed of changes in the patient's condition, which could range from the serious, such as an impending respiratory insufficiency, to the more frequent and routine, such as the need for a pain med or a change in a patient's diet. Many interactions with physicians over medical orders were not problematic, but others required that the RN actively engage in negotiating changes that the doctor might not readily agree to, but that the RN believed necessary due to her greater proximity to the patient (more continuous observation), the risk involved (an impending respiratory or cardiac arrest), or a greater familiarity with a patient's needs (the dosage of a pain med). There was always the possibility for misunderstandings and for differing interpretations of patients' needs. However, nurses were required to keep physicians informed; hence it was particularly irritating to RNs when doctors were rude or acted annoyed. Nurses frequently complained to each other about unappreciative physicians and developed strategies for handling them.

As the patient moved through their "illness trajectory," if the conditions that led to their hospitalization were eliminated or controlled at a level acceptable to the physician, the doctor ordered the patient to be discharged or transferred to a convalescent facility. In cases where the patient did not improve but ultimately "expired," this event did not officially take place (although nurses may have witnessed it) until the attending physician or a medical colleague determined that it had and documented it in the patient's chart. After the physician's pronouncement, the RN performed the "dirty work" of post-mortem care [43].

When patients were discharged, their hospitalization ended with the same division of labor that structured the admission. The physician ordered the discharge, the medications and treatments the patient was to continue at home, and any follow-up office visits. The doctor might ask the primary nurse how the patient was feeling, but he certainly did not ask the RN to concur in the decision. Once the discharge order was written, the primary nurse discontinued the medical orders and coordinated the patient's departure, making sure the take home medications were procured from the pharmacy and that the patient was ready when the transportation aide arrived to escort them to the entrance of the hospital. Nursing care usually ended when the patient exited the ward, but if the escort service did not show up, the RN's work could even include transporting the patient and helping them into a vehicle for the ride home.

As essential as RNs were to patient care, doctors did not treat RNs as professional colleagues. Nursing educators had argued that without auxiliaries at the bedside, physicians would seek out the professional nurse and communicate directly about the care of the patient, as physicians commonly do with their medical colleagues [44]. RNs did go about their work with considerable autonomy, but as I have described, their work remained within a subordinate work jurisdiction over which physicians maintained professional dominance through critical decisions and medical orders. Sometimes physicians did seek out the primary nurse when there was a particular problem; however, they did not usually discuss the case in detail and often did not even question the nurse regarding the patient's condition, preferring to make their own assessment. In day-to-day activity on the wards, nurses who wished to consult with doctors often had to stalk them through the ward or leave notes on the front of patients' charts, as physicians frequently visited patients and left medical orders without communicating with the primary nurse at all. Doctors also gave verbal orders to the charge nurse and occasionally even to the ward clerk to be communicated to the patient's nurse. And, while doctors did read the technical data documented in the patient's chart, they frequently skipped the "nurses' notes" section, that is, the nurse's ongoing assessment of the patient's condition.

Rather than elevate RNs to colleagueship with physicians, primary nursing reinforced their accountability. If medical orders were not properly carried out, physicians could initiate administrative investigations of RNs' work, and without auxiliaries mediating between the RN and the patient, there was no longer any ambiguity as to who was responsible for carrying out specific tasks. RNs were individually accountable for the complete care of patients. In addition, although RNs voluntarily filed hospital "incident reports" when they discovered their own errors, when doctors discovered such errors they pursued the problem directly with the primary nurse, the shift charge nurse, or the unit manager. In some cases, doctors demanded that an incident report be filled out. Primary nurses then initiated investigations of their own work performance on behalf of physicians. In contrast, although RNs often complained about physicians' rudeness, inadequacies, and even errors, they did so informally with other staff members. Verbal complaints were not communicated directly to physicians, and I never heard of any formal written complaints. Rather, RNs helped physicians avoid mistakes by drawing problems to their attention, sometimes reminding them of what needed to be done.

Thus, although the displacement of auxiliaries facilitated RNs' exercise of responsibility, because RNs occupied a subordinate work jurisdiction, the flattening of the nursing hierarchy augmented their accountability as well. Consequently, physicians never mounted a campaign to defeat the implementation of primary nursing—the reorganization of nursing work was never a threat to their professional dominance.

Bureaucratic Control

As Pacific Hospital reorganized into a diversified health care corporation and implemented new procedures for controlling costs, all workers were subject to greater bureaucratic control. With the growth of managerial functions, even physicians' sphere of power was more limited. Nonetheless, as we have seen, physicians continued to participate in the governance of the corporation and to dominate nurses and the medical division of labor [45]. In contrast, RNs were subject to much greater administrative control.

Bureaucratic control of RNs began prior to their actual engagement in labor, as nurses were subject to managerial rules dictating the terms of employment: the shift, hours, wages, and job requirements. In accepting a position, an RN formally agreed to hospital personnel policies specifying scheduling, rest and meal breaks, documenting time cards, and a detailed job description of tasks and responsibilities that included rules regarding the nurse's uniform and norms for conduct while on duty.

Bureaucratic rules also guided the performance of RNs' labor on the wards. RNs could not carry out their work without an extensive knowledge of hospital rules and procedures. Policies existed for the admission and discharge of the patient, the performance of many nursing care tasks, the documentation of that care, and even the sequential placement of forms in the patient's chart. There were rules for answering the patient's call light, taking vital signs, calling the doctor, and a variety of other tasks, including the ordering of support services from their respective departments. RNs followed hospital protocols for transfusing blood, administering medications, performing post-operative care, "coding" the patient who arrested, and for other nursing procedures.

Although bureaucratic rules continued to proliferate with corporatization, ironically, administrative control of RNs' labor was strengthened through the *elimination* of rules that had been established in team nursing. With the conversion to primary nursing, rules that had differentiated tasks among RNs, LPNs, and nurses' aides were no longer needed. In fact, the complexity of these rules and their frequent violation had compromised the effectiveness of bureaucratic control [46]. As tasks were reunified and the nursing hierarchy flattened, RNs were unambiguously responsible for carrying out total patient care according to hospital policies and procedures. RNs had gained control over the work they were responsible for, but in doing so they were now more accountable to management as well as to physicians.

The reunification of tasks also changed the character of bureaucratic infractions. Because work was intensified, some rules were commonly violated, but management did not enforce them because the hospital benefitted by ignoring the infractions. For example, RNs routinely breached rules regarding rest and meal breaks. They were supposed to take a ten minute break every two hours and a thirty minute meal break every four hours, but it was very difficult for nurses to take their breaks on time, if at all. Because the violation of these rules facilitated getting the work done without overtime costs, they were not enforced [47]. In some cases unit managers actually encouraged staff nurses to violate rules, concealing the effects of work intensification. Staff nurses on one ward confided that their unit manager suggested RNs avoid recording overtime because it would hurt the ward's budget and be detrimental when higher management compared their unit with other wards. Informants confided that under a new management incentive program, unit managers received a bonus if ward expenses were under budget. Similar pressures existed on each shift as charge nurses as well suggested RNs be conservative in recording overtime so their shift would not look bad when the unit manager reviewed time cards.

Rule violations did not always work to the advantage of management. Shift charge nurses were closely aligned with staff nurses and violated hospital rules themselves in attempting to protect their overloaded staff from additional work. In some cases, charge nurses openly argued that the work load made conditions unsafe for patients. Charge nurses were also able to regulate the amount of work on their shift by influencing the disposition and timing of patient admissions, transfers, and discharges. During busy shifts, I observed charge nurses who subtly delayed admissions, postponed transfers until the next shift, or manipulated nursing administrators or physicians into admitting or transferring patients to other wards [48].

Furthermore, staff nurses violated bureaucratic rules when trying to deal with the effects of job enlargement. When nurses were overloaded with doctors' orders and patient demands, or experiencing inadequate staffing or support services, they sometimes broke hospital rules in an attempt to regain control over their work. There were even instances in which RNs charted tasks that had not actually been performed. In one case, rather than take routine vital signs, the nurse simply charted entries similar to those she had entered four hours earlier. Although the patient was in stable condition and not seriously ill, this type of deviance was considered unethical and a risky means of regaining control over work. More often, as I discussed earlier, RNs simply omitted what they considered time-consuming tasks of lesser importance. Or, if the task could not be omitted or shifted to the patient, they passed it on to the next shift. The RN may not have had time to walk the patient or to give a complete daily bath, so she simply explained to the nurse on the next shift that she was unable to get the task accomplished. However, to avoid resentment, nurses often "stayed over" to perform the tasks on unpaid overtime or paid overtime, if they felt it could be justified.

As I have shown, primary nursing failed to upgrade RNs' work or elevate them to a more prestigious position. Rather, RNs' work was intensified and their accountability to both physicians and administrators augmented. Despite primary nursing's ideology of professional upgrading, structural change in the social relations of production remained confined to the reduction if not elimination of a paranursing hierarchy on hospital wards. Thus, when contrasting the observations of sociologists writing in the team nursing period with my own observations of primary nursing, I was struck not only by the reversal in the division of labor but by the durability of the larger institutional and occupational hierarchy. Pacific Hospital had transformed itself into a diversified health care corporation and reorganized the division of labor on hospital wards, yet the structural inequality between elites and subordinate workers remained.

The Limits of Cooperation, Workers' Disunity, and the Empowerment of RNs

Although the reorganization of work did not enable RNs to challenge physicians' professional dominance or managers' bureaucratic control, the intensification of work ultimately undermined RNs' consent. RNs had cooperated in the reorganization of work during the 1970s and the first half of the 1980s, but in the latter part of the decade feelings of dissatisfaction were running high. An RN with years of experience on the wards expressed the sentiments of many workers when she declared that "Pacific is now a big business, not a community hospital." Since the mid-1970s, what was originally a community hospital with a relatively small and paternalistic administration had reorganized into a commercially diversified corporation and intensified labor on the hospital's wards and in support departments. When labor contracts were again due to expire, many workers recognized that their work problems were linked with the changing political economy of the industry and that any savings due to the hospital's intensification of work was likely to flow into the development of new businesses and corporate administrative costs.

Feelings of dissatisfaction throughout the hospital provided a basis for workers to collectively resist deteriorating working conditions. Nurses were increasingly discontented with work on the wards although they weren't sure what to do about it. Nonprofessional service workers had also experienced intensified labor, but without any claim to upgrading and status enhancement. Although RNs and service workers were divided somewhat by social class and race, the majority of workers were women, and this common gender identity cut across occupational distinctions, providing another basis for unity.

Nevertheless, just as primary nursing had contradictory effects on RNs' work (overcoming the problems of team nursing while intensifying labor), the reorganization of the labor process also had contradictory effects on hospital workers' solidarity. The displacement of auxiliaries from nursing wards weakened the possibility of a larger hospital-wide solidarity by distancing RNs from remaining nonprofessional workers, who were now concentrated in support departments. As discussed earlier, the intensification of work strained relations with these workers, dispersing tension laterally. However, while weakening a larger solidarity among workers, the displacement of auxiliaries empowered RNs in collective bargaining by eliminating their vulnerability to substitution [49]. These contradictions were manifest during contract negotiations and an RN strike in 1987.

A divided work force was clearly evident from the beginning of contract negotiations in 1987. Although both the Service Employees International Union (SEIU) local and the California Nurses' Association (CNA) represented the more liberal and progressive segments of their respective national organizations, as discussed in Chapter 2, the history of relations between them involved minimal cooperation and even underlying antagonism. While RNs had walked the picket line during the San Francisco RN strike of 1974, auxiliary nurses and other service workers had continued to work. Similarly, RNs had worked during a strike by auxiliary nurses and service workers in 1979. Throughout the postwar period and into the 1980s, both the union and the CNA failed to pursue mutually expiring contracts and, again in 1987, both organizations engaged in independent negotiations.

Pacific's corporate management entered negotiations with the SEIU local in the spring, claiming financial deficits and demanding major concessions in wages and benefits. As with negotiations in 1983 and 1985 (see Chapter 2), rank and file efforts to address issues regarding the work speedup were overshadowed by management's demands on wages and benefits and the union's defensive response. SEIU claimed that Pacific Hospital and other area hospitals currently engaged in negotiations were "above the national average and the state norm in terms of profitability and capital," but nonprofessional workers were in a weak bargaining position. Taking advantage of the segmented labor market that existed between professional and nonprofessional workers, management treated service workers as though they were expendable. In addition, the union was internally divided, the entrenched leadership having failed to effectively address issues of concern to rank and file unionists. A grassroots challenge by activists had resulted in national union leaders placing the local in trusteeship, which demobilized rank and file workers during contract negotiations. Furthermore, service workers at Pacific Hospital were divided over the wisdom of striking. Many felt the 1979 strike had failed to achieve substantial gains. The labor movement as a whole was on the defensive, and workers, feeling vulnerable, wanted to hold onto their jobs and the wage and benefit improvements they had attained in the 1960s and 1970s. A week before the contract expired, service workers at two other regional hospitals represented by the union settled their negotiations without a strike. Shortly afterward, negotiators at Pacific Hospital reached a similar agreement. Major concessions were again avoided; however, wage increases were limited to a total of 7 percent over the next three years, ensuring that real wages were likely to remain flat or even decline over the contract period. Work problems originating in the reorganization and intensification of labor continued to be neglected [50].

Meanwhile, CNA leaders were mobilizing for their own negotiations, which led to an impasse with management in the summer of 1987. Because RNs had become greatly dissatisfied with the increased work load on the wards, they were not only asking for a significant wage increase of 14 percent over two years but also for staffing by "acuity," that is, by the severity of patients' medical-nursing needs as opposed to assigning a specific number of patients to each nurse. Management countered with a proposed wage increase comparable to that accepted by nonprofessional workers, demands for concessions on seniority rights, and a proposal that charge nurses be taken out of collective bargaining representation and reclassified as exempt managerial employees [51].

Negotiations at several other area hospitals represented by the CNA were taking place simultaneously. A week prior to the strike at Pacific, RNs at one hospital reached an agreement that included a wage increase of 10 percent over two years, while RNs at another hospital went on strike. With negotiations at Pacific stalled, approximately 1000 RNs walked out several days later. A CNA spokesperson accurately summarized the strike issue in stating that on hospital wards there were "fewer nurses, sicker patients and more work." For a week, RNs walked the picket line, overcoming the isolation of working on different wards and shifts and finding strength in their mutual grievances [52].

The intensification of work was the major strike issue for rank and file RNs, however there was a tendency for work dissatisfaction to be displaced into bargaining over wages. This was clearly evident when CNA spokespersons justified their demand for a 14 percent wage increase over two years by the increased work load on the wards. The chief negotiator for the CNA even stated that RNs were "willing to work with management to make the work more efficient, but to retain nurses they must be adequately compensated." The leadership's emphasis on wages was a questionable strategy given the relatively good wages of RNs in the San Francisco Bay area. Pacific Hospital's RNs, like Bay area nurses generally, were among the highest paid in the nation, an advantage resulting from their organization for collective bargaining [53]. To justify a significant pay increase based on the increased intensity of the labor process was to propose an economistic trading of higher wages for RNs' cooperation in management's efforts to increase the work load.

Although the displacement of auxiliaries had weakened SEIU's organization of hospital workers and the possibility of a larger work-place solidarity, it actually empowered RNs by eliminating their vulnerability to substitution by auxiliaries. Because the vast majority of auxiliary nurses had been displaced from the hospital's wards, management was no longer able to replace striking RNs with LPNs and nurses' aides, eliminating RNs' "functional redundancy" [54]. Managers tried to keep the hospital functioning by staffing with nurse administrators and the small number of remaining LPNs, but because this did not provide enough labor power to maintain an adequate patient census, the hospital started bringing in some temporary RNs through a nationwide staffing agency. These strikebreakers were housed inside the hospital and paid wages double that of staff RNs, infuriating nurses and confirming their worst views of the management style that had come into existence with corporatization. Management's action strengthened RNs' determination on the picket line, which was now reinforced by RNs from other hospitals as well. In addition, several unions made public statements supporting the CNA, and teamsters honored the picket line by unloading deliveries of supplies on the sidewalk outside the hospital and refusing to pick up the hospital's garbage. However, the real strength of the strike remained the unity among RNs, who were now the critical work force on the hospital's wards [55].

The strike was soon effective. After several days, the hospital's census was reduced to 25 percent of available beds. Management then laid off 400 service workers in admitting, food service, laundry, and housekeeping. Most of these workers were represented by SEIU, which after settling its own negotiations earlier, had maintained a low visibility throughout the strike. Meanwhile, another competing hospital outside the Pacific system settled with CNA, avoiding a strike. With Pacific Hospital losing money daily, negotiations resumed a week after the strike began, and a settlement was quickly reached. RNs attained a 10 percent wage increase over two years and to the surprise of many nurses, management agreed to staffing by acuity. Experienced RNs were skeptical as the CNA had attempted before to gain greater participation in setting staffing guidelines. The 1974 strike had resulted in the establishment of "professional performance committees," which had cooperated with management without effectively resisting the intensification of work in subsequent years. This history suggested that, although management had agreed to implement some type of staffing by acuity, substantive changes to reduce the intensity of labor would likely be met with counterstrategies by the corporation. Nevertheless, RNs had resisted concessions and made gains that would have been unlikely if they had remained vulnerable to substitution by auxiliaries.

RNs were justified in their skepticism of corporate management. After they returned to the wards, executives announced a 3 percent budget cut and revealed that Pacific Hospital would merge with a nearby hospital the corporation was acquiring. Some service lines would be consolidated, and workers feared that this might lead to staff reductions. In addition, staffing by acuity continued to be a contested process, with RNs pointing out that managers controlled the joint committee established to implement the change. A committee member and informant communicated that "being on the committee feels more like serving management than nurses. The committee is bringing acuity data into line with management's staffing guidelines."

RNs feared that their work load would never be significantly reduced, but in the following year management introduced an important change. The recent strike had made it clear that the intensity of work was seriously undermining RNs' cooperation. To alleviate continued dissatisfaction on the wards as well as offset a growing shortage of RNs, administrators announced that the hospital was implementing pilot studies to reintroduce some nurses' aides back onto the wards. Administrators carefully avoided the use of the term "team nursing" and reassured RNs that a small number of "nursing assistants" on each ward would not replace RNs or interfere with their professional care at the bedside. An informant in administration confided management's hopes that if "patient care assistants" helped with the many low-level tasks, productivity gains could be sustained while undercutting RNs' dissatisfaction and demands for larger salary increases. The hospital had moved too far toward implementing an all-RN work force.

NOTES

1. The nursing literature on primary nursing is enormous. Major works include Gwen D. Marram, Margaret W. Schlegel, and Em O. Bevis, *Primary Nursing: A Model for Individualized Care* (St. Louis: C. V. Mosby Company, 1974); Marie Manthey, *The Practice of Primary Nursing* (Boston: Blackwell Scientific Publications, 1980); Mary O'Neil Mundinger,

Autonomy in Nursing (Germantown, Md.: Aspen, 1980); Karen S. Zander, *Primary Nursing: Development and Management* (Germantown, Md.: Aspen, 1980); Carl Joiner and Gwen Marram van Servellen, *Job Enrichment in Nursing* (Rockville, Md.: Aspen, 1984).

2. See Manthey, *Practice of Primary Nursing*, chap. 1; Joiner and van Servellen, *Job Enrichment in Nursing*, chap. 2, 3. An advocate of primary nursing commented that "what bastardized team concepts was . . . the stamping of a label ["team nursing"] . . . on to a task-oriented [functional] assignment organization." Genrose J. Alfano, ed., *The All-RN Nursing Staff* (Wakefield, Mass.: Nursing Resources, 1980), 57.

3. Marie Manthey et al., "Primary Nursing: A Return to the Concept of 'My Nurse' and 'My Patient,'" *Nursing Forum* 9(1) (1970): 77. Actually, in team nursing, *formal* responsibility for patient care was never shared with auxiliaries. However, auxiliaries' position at the bedside provided an experience of responsibility that competed with RNs' formal responsibility. See my discussion in chap. 4.

4. Manthey et al., "Primary Nursing," 64-83 for further discussion of these points; also sources in n. 1.

5. Manthey et al., "Primary Nursing." Some of the basic ideas of primary nursing preceded the formulation by Manthey and her associates. McClure and Nelson mention a growing interest in returning RNs to bedside care at Montefiore Hospital in New York in the early 1960s. Margaret L. McClure and M. Janice Nelson, "Trends in Hospital Nursing," in *Nursing in the 1980s: Crisis, Opportunities, Challenges*, ed. Linda H. Aiken (Philadelphia: J. B. Lippincott, 1982), 67. Similarly, Luther P. Christman and Richard C. Jelinek suggested that auxiliary staffing be reduced in "Old Patterns Waste Half the Nursing Hours," *The Modern Hospital* 108(1) (Jan. 1967): 78-81.

6. Lambertsen had raised the same objection to the use of the case method with auxiliary nurses in the immediate postwar period. Team nursing had been developed in part to overcome this problem. See my discussion of the development of team nursing in chap. 4.

7. Alfano, *All-RN Nursing Staff*.

8. Luther Christman, "A Micro-Analysis of the Nursing Division of One Medical Center," in *Nursing Personnel and the Changing Health Care System*, ed. Michael L. Millman (Cambridge, Mass.: Ballinger, 1978), table 8-1.

9. For example, at Family Hospital in Milwaukee between 1973 and 1978, the nursing work force was reorganized from 29 percent RNs and 71 percent auxiliaries to the opposite of 77 percent RNs and 23 percent auxiliaries. In 1973, LPNs comprised 16 percent of Family Hospital's nursing workers and nurses' aides 55 percent, but by 1978 LPNs had been reduced to 5 percent and nurses' aides to 18 percent. Barbara J. Brown, "Reorganizing Hospital-Based Nursing Practice: An Analysis of Patient Outcomes,

Provider Satisfaction, and Costs," in *Health Policy and Nursing Practice*, ed. Linda H. Aiken (New York: McGraw-Hill, 1981), 125, 135. As I indicated in chap. 2, many auxiliaries were shifted to peripheral work sites as hospital corporations diversified.

10. Under current arrangements in most hospitals, a patient's bed assignment is handled by nursing administration based on bed availability and the doctor's diagnosis, not on an effort to maintain continuity in each nurse's patient assignment. If primary nursing were to ever overcome this problem, it could still be argued that RNs' responsibility should extend to subsequent admissions of the patient, as it typically does for physicians. This, of course, is even more impractical.

11. The American Nurses' Association reports that over 30 percent of employed nurses work on a part-time basis. See American Nurses' Association, *Facts About Nursing, 86-87* (Kansas City: American Nurses' Association, 1987), table 1.6 and 1.7.

12. Many of these issues were explained to me by nurses at Pacific Hospital, but they were also debated in the nursing literature. For discussion of variation in primary nursing see Karen L. Ciske, "Accountability: The Essence of Primary Nursing," *American Journal of Nursing* (May 1979): 891-894; Alfano, *All-RN Nursing Staff*, 49-58; Gwen Marram van Servellen, "Primary Nursing: Variations in Practice," *The Journal of Nursing Administration* (Sept. 1981): 40-46; Joiner and van Servellen, *Job Enrichment in Nursing*, 25-30.

13. Alfano, *The All-RN Nursing Staff*.

14. For discussions of nursing shortages in the 1980s, see Linda H. Aiken and Robert J. Blendon, "The National Nurse Shortage," *National Journal* (23 May 1981): 948-953; Linda H. Aiken, Robert J. Blendon, David E. Rogers, "The Shortage of Hospital Nurses: A New Perspective," *American Journal of Nursing* (Sept. 1981): 1612-1618; and Margaret L. McClure, "The Inconsistent Supply of Professionally Qualified Nurses," in *All-RN Nursing Staff*, ed. Alfano, 65-68; *New York Times*, 7 July 1987, p. 1.

15. Debates have appeared in a variety of nursing journals, including the following: Marie Manthey, "Can Primary Nursing Survive?," *American Journal of Nursing* (May 1988): 644-647; Joyce C. Clifford, "Will the Professional Practice Model Survive?," *Journal of Professional Nursing* 4(2) (1988): 77.

16. Andrew Abbott, *The System of Professions* (Chicago: University of Chicago Press, 1988), 72.

17. Ibid., 118. Also, Andrew Abbott, "Status and Status Strain in the Professions," *American Journal of Sociology* 86(4) (1981): 819-835.

18. In the 1982-83 academic year, during the peak years of the transition to RN-predominant staffing, 15% of RN graduates received degrees from hospital diploma programs, 31% from baccalaureate programs, and 54% from associate degree programs. In contrast, during the 1965-66 academic

year, at the height of team nursing, 75% received degrees from hospital diploma programs, 15.5% from baccalaureate programs, and only 9.5% from community colleges. American Nurses' Association, *Facts About Nursing, 84-85* (American Nurses' Association: Kansas City, 1985), table 2.6. Data from 1965-66 academic year calculated from McClure and Nelson, "Trends in Hospital Nursing," table 4-3.

19. On the role of community colleges in American society, see Jerome Karabel, "Community Colleges and Social Stratification," *Harvard Educational Review* 42(6) (Nov. 1972): 521-562. For a discussion of the weak linkage between credentialing and work requirements, see my discussion of RNs' vulnerability to substitution in chap. 4.

20. See sources in n. 1. Also, Gwen Marram van Servellen and Mychelle M. Mowry, "DRGs and Primary Nursing: Are They Compatible?," *The Journal of Nursing Administration* (Apr. 1985): 32-36.

21. As Richard Edwards points out, "de-skilling and the increasing use of low-skill, low-wage labor is only one avenue for reducing unit costs. . . . It may pay the firm to pay a wage higher than the least possible wage if the result is a more than proportionate increase in productivity." "The Social Relations of Production at the Point of Production," *The Insurgent Sociologist* 8(2/3) (Fall 1978): 110-111.

22. Aiken and Blendon, "National Nurse Shortage"; Aiken, Blendon, and Rogers, "Shortages of Hospital Nurses"; Linda H. Aiken, "The Nurse Labor Market," *Health Affairs* 1(4) (Fall 1982): 30-40; Linda Aiken, "Breaking the Shortage Cycles," *American Journal of Nursing* (Dec. 1987): 1616-1620.

23. For discussions that rely on a view of professionalism as false consciousness, see John Ehrenreich and Barbara Ehrenreich, "Hospital Workers: A Case Study of 'The New Working Class,'" *Monthly Review* 24(8) (Jan. 1973): 12-27; Boston Nurses' Group, "The False Promise: Professionalism in Nursing," *Science for the People* 10 (May/June 1978): 20-34; (July/Aug. 1978): 23-33.

24. On one medical ward the day shift was staffed with 14 RNs and 1 LPN, the p.m. shift with 12 RNs and 2 LPNs, and the night shift with 9 RNs and 2 LPNs. As I mentioned in chapter 2, some of the last nurses' aides to work on the hospital's wards were transferred to employment in a newly acquired rehabilitation hospital in the mid-1980s. Although the official policy of the hospital stated that LPNs were nonprofessional nursing workers subordinate to RNs, LPNs had their own patient assignments and engaged in the complete care of patients, with few exceptions. They were prohibited from administering IVs, from transfusing blood, and from inserting nasogastric tubes. These tasks were not beyond the ability of LPNs, however they were restricted by formal job descriptions and organized nursing's power to define licensing and practice criteria. In addition, LPNs did not wish to compete with RNs to perform these tasks. LPNs felt they were already taken advantage of because for the most part

they performed the same work as RNs, yet were paid less and had lower status. In addition, starting IVs and transfusing blood could be frustrating and time consuming, and because of AIDS, workers were concerned that these tasks placed them more at risk.

25. Hospital statistical data on personnel was not available to me. However, my estimate of credentialing levels was confirmed by informants in middle management. In addition, ANA data indicates that associate and hospital diploma degree RNs constituted the majority of staff RNs nationally and in the geographical area in which Pacific Hospital is located. American Nurses' Association, *Facts About Nursing, 84-85*, table 1.27.

26. In contrast, for discussions of the importance of status in professional occupations see Magali Sarfatti Larson, *The Rise of Professionalism* (Berkeley: University of California Press, 1977); Abbott, "Status and Status Strain."

27. Fred E. Katz, "Nurses," in *The Semi-Professions and Their Organization: Teachers, Nurses, Social Workers,* ed. Amitai Etzioni (New York: Free Press, 1969), 73.

28. Eliot Freidson discusses professionalism among paraprofessionals in *Profession of Medicine* (New York: Dodd, Mead, 1970; Chicago: University of Chicago Press, 1988), chap. 3.

29. The shift charge nurse frequently had a small patient assignment and when she had a day off other RNs took turns being in charge.

30. For a discussion of shift report as nursing ritual, see Zane Robinson Wolf, *Nurses' Work: The Sacred and the Profane* (Philadelphia: University of Pennsylvania Press, 1988), chap. 5.

31. New RNs frequently found it difficult to develop the required organizational skills, which were learned informally on the job rather than in credentialing programs.

32. For a discussion of emotional labor, see Arlie Hochschild, *The Managed Heart* (Berkeley: University of California Press, 1983). For a related discussion of "comfort" and "sentimental" work in medical settings, see Anselm Strauss et al., *Social Organization of Medical Work* (Chicago: University of Chicago Press, 1985), chap. 5 and 6.

33. For a discussion of nursing rituals involved in avoiding medication errors, see Wolf, *Nurses' Work*, chap. 3.

34. See chap. 2 for a discussion of the effects of cost control on hospitals.

35. The orderly's position was later reinstated after a significant rise in RNs' back injuries on the p.m. shift.

36. Team nursing may have helped ease relations with nonprofessional service workers because LPNs and nurses' aides often socialized with these workers during breaks and sometimes outside the workplace, whereas RNs rarely did so. With the displacement of auxiliary nurses, class and status differences between RNs and nonprofessional workers were accentuated, contributing to RNs' difficulties in coordinating support services.

In the mid-1980s Pacific implemented a computer-based system that decreased face-to-face and telephone interaction between ward RNs and peripheral department workers. While tension still existed between RNs and ancillary workers, relations became more impersonal and bureaucratic. For a discussion of the "dispersion of conflict" in a factory setting in which operatives were dependent upon ancillary workers, see Michael Burawoy, *Manufacturing Consent: Changes in the Labor Process under Monopoly Capitalism* (Chicago: University of Chicago Press, 1979).

37. For an important study of how work has also been shifted from wage labor in health care institutions to unpaid labor in households, see Nona Y. Glazer, "Overlooked, Overworked: Women's Unpaid and Paid Work in the Health Services' 'Cost Crisis,'" *International Journal of Health Services* 18(1) (1988): 119-137; Glazer, "The Home as Workshop: Women as Amateur Nurses and Medical Care Providers," *Gender and Society* 4(4) (1990): 479-499. Glazer argues that the shift from paid to unpaid women workers is a managerial strategy to reduce labor costs, and that the "dewaging" of women's labor is a general trend reversing the commodification of services once produced in the household. According to Glazer, the strategy is not limited to health care and includes the development of self-service in retail sales. Glazer, "Servants to Capital: Unpaid Domestic Labor and Paid Work," *Review of Radical Political Economics* 16(1) (1984): 61-87.

In contrast, I am concerned specifically with the shift from paid to unpaid work *within the hospital*. In addition, although primary nursing restructured the division of labor between RNs' paid labor and patient/family members' unpaid work, at Pacific Hospital this change was initiated informally by staff nurses as a means of handling the greater intensity of the work process. Furthermore, there were important constraints on the shifting of work onto patients and their families.

Finally, in my discussion on the reorganization of the industry in Part One I indicate that the "decommodification" of health care services has taken place within a larger context of *commodifying* the institutional periphery of hospitals by creating a host of diversified new businesses. This is a major reason why the shift of services to the periphery has not been an effective means of cost control. Hospitals have reorganized into diversified corporations to capture revenues from non-acute care settings, including home care. See chap. 2.

38. Judith Lorber, "Good Patients and Problem Patients: Conformity and Deviance in a General Hospital," *Journal of Health and Social Behavior* 16(2) (1975): 220.

39. Of course, patient (client) participation remains an important part of the work process. For a study that emphasizes patient participation in medical-nursing work, see Strauss et al., *Social Organization of Medical Work*, particularly chap. 8. While full of insights, the approach of the

authors neglects historical changes in the organization of nursing work on hospital wards.

40. Ibid., 26, 155.

41. Abbott notes that the "current concept of 'nursing diagnosis' embraces nearly every aspect of well-being. It will for that reason be untenable." *System of Professions*, 347, n. 38.

42. Unit managers usually overlooked incomplete care plans. The one time their completion was stressed was just before the annual inspection by the Joint Commission on the Accreditation of Hospitals.

43. In cases where death had been expected for some time, the nursing supervisor could pronounce the patient dead, but only by the delegated authority of the physician and under a specific order authorizing her to do so. For a discussion of nurses' post-mortem care, see Wolf, *Nurses' Work*, chap. 2.

44. See Manthey et al., "Primary Nursing," 72.

45. See chap. 2 for a discussion of changes in the governing tripartite of Pacific Hospital and Corporation.

46. See discussion in chap. 4.

47. In contrast, administrators periodically cracked down on infractions of the dress code and other minor rules that reinforced their control over nurses.

48. Of course, to the extent that the informal regulatory activities of charge nurses did reduce possible harmful effects on patients, they may have contributed to protecting not only staff nurses, but the larger organization from the worst effects of work intensification.

49. I discussed RNs' vulnerability to substitution by auxiliaries during the team nursing period in chap. 4.

50. Unless otherwise cited, all discussion is based on participant observations, interviews with informants, and data from local newspaper accounts which I have not identified in order to maintain the anonymity of Pacific Hospital and its workers. For a larger discussion of labor relations within the industry during this period, see Leon Fink and Brian Greenberg, *Upheaval in the Quiet Zone* (Urbana: University of Illinois Press, 1989); Karen Brodkin Sacks, *Caring by the Hour* (Urbana: University of Illinois Press, 1988).

51. Unit managers were already exempt from collective bargaining. Management's efforts to exclude shift charge nurses from CNA representation was part of a managerial effort to use first-line supervisors to inhibit RNs' organization.

52. For a discussion of workers' solidarity in strikes and collective action, see Rick Fantasia, *Cultures of Solidarity* (Berkeley: University of California Press, 1988). Fantasia's work contains an interesting case study of a unionization drive at Springfield Hospital in Vermont. Although RNs at Pacific Hospital were already organized for collective bargaining,

solidarity is problematic in any effort to engage in effective collective action.

53. This is not to say that RNs did not deserve a pay increase. CNA research staff indicated that "the big gains were made in the 60's, when women in general and RNs in particular began to fight for equitable pay." Negotiators argued that since the early 1970s, real wages had barely kept pace with inflation. For data on differences in RNs' wages regionally, see American Nurses' Association, *Facts About Nursing, 84-85*, tables 3.3 and 3.4.

54. The term "functional redundancy" is from Margaret Levi, "Functional Redundancy and the Process of Professionalization: The Case of Registered Nurses in the United States," *Journal of Health Politics, Policy and Law* 5(2) (Summer 1980): 333-353.

55. Although SEIU workers had continued to work, some were sympathetic, feeling at this time that it was in their interest to support RNs in order to hold up their own wages and benefits. However, segmented labor markets had a negative impact as nonprofessional workers generally resented the fact that RNs were likely to gain a wage increase that exceeded the 7 percent service workers had settled for.

CHAPTER 6

Conclusion and Epilogue

This study has focused on the reorganization of nursing during the cost containment decades of the 1970s and 1980s. In explaining the reorganization of nurses' work, I have attempted to link changes on hospital wards with changes in the political economy of the industry and the corporatization of hospitals. I began with the growing contradiction between the continued expansion of the industry and slower growth in the larger political economy, a contradiction that has forced non-health care capital and the state to pressure providers to control costs. In response, community hospitals reorganized for survival and continued expansion. The role of corporate managers grew in importance, but physicians' power suffered only a relative decline as managers, physicians, and trustees continued to dominate a work force of subordinate workers. When management introduced more rationalized systems to control labor costs and increase productivity, nonprofessional workers were subject to a speedup and closer supervision. In contrast, although nurses were also subject to work intensification, their credentialing was upgraded and their work jurisdiction and responsibility were enlarged.

During the cost containment era of the 1970s and 1980s, nursing work on hospital wards was reorganized from a division of labor that included stratified workers (RNs and auxiliaries) performing differentiated tasks to one in which RNs perform reunified tasks in an unmediated relationship with their patients. Despite the importance of managerial interest in increasing productivity, I have argued that the reorganization of the division of labor cannot be understood from this perspective alone. In fact, primary nursing was developed and promoted by an elite of nursing educators and administrators as a strategy to further nursing's professionalization. In doing so, nursing leaders claimed that team nursing and the subdivision of labor in the 1950s and 1960s had deprofessionalized the occupation, an argument that corresponds with sociological theories of proletarianization. In reunifying tasks and the RN-patient relationship, primary nursing was supposedly based on principles of professional practice that had existed in private duty nursing before RNs' employment in hospitals.

In contrast, I have argued that the transition from team to primary nursing contradicts major theories of both professionalization and proletarianization. Through a comparative study of the organization of nursing labor that combined the use of historical sources, prior sociological studies of team nursing, and observations on the wards of Pacific Hospital, I have maintained that the nursing labor process has varied dramatically, both differentiating and reunifying tasks at the same time that RNs have remained a semiprofession subordinate to administrators and physicians.

To assess the claim that team nursing deprofessionalized nursing and that primary nursing reprofessionalizes the occupation by returning to organizational principles that existed before RNs' employment in hospitals, I began Part Two with an examination of hospital apprenticeship and private duty. Before the Great Depression, hospital nursing was organized around an apprenticeship system that was based on the exploitation of unpaid labor and maintained through the authoritarianism of hospitals and training schools. In private duty nursing, graduate nurses were free of institutional domination, but subject to the coercion of an open labor market and the tyranny of employment in private households. Rather than constitute professional practice, nurses' unmediated relationship with the client enabled the patient as both the employer and consumer of services to exercise considerable power over graduate nurses' work. In addition, nurses' responsibility for patients' "complete care" created an occupational jurisdiction so open-ended that it could include housework, creating a marginal distinction between graduate nurses, practical nurses, and domestic servant labor.

In reinterpreting sociological studies of team nursing conducted in the immediate postwar period, I discussed the complexity of this organizational form, which upgraded RNs' tasks and responsibility at the same time that RNs were subordinated in a hospital-based labor process. Team nursing was developed by industry and nursing elites to organize a stratified work force of RNs and auxiliaries. The differentiation of tasks appeared compatible both with managerial interests in subdividing the work process and occupational interests in professionalizing RNs' work by delegating routine tasks to nonprofessional workers. Nevertheless, RNs were neither fully professionalized nor technically proletarianized, that is, deskilled. While scientific management principles were applied to differentiate nursing tasks, when compared with prior forms of nursing labor, clearly RNs' work, responsibility, and autonomy were upgraded. RNs' dissatisfaction originated in the contradictions of team nursing rather than in the successful application of scientific management principles, as is commonly claimed by advocates of primary nursing and suggested by theories of deprofessionalization or technical proletarianization. Although subdividing work on the wards divided workers and adversely affected team integration, the major problems of team nursing resulted from RNs' vulnerability to substitution by auxiliaries, whose more continuous presence at the bedside empowered them and provided a competing experience of responsibility that complicated RNs' formal authority and accountability.

Primary nursing and total patient care were developed by nursing leaders dissatisfied with the large numbers of auxiliaries on the wards and the failure of RNs to attain full professional status. While maintaining that team nursing had deprofessionalized the occupation, nursing educators argued that reunified tasks and an unmediated relationship with patients would reprofessionalize RNs' work. As I have discussed, variants of primary nursing with a majority of RNs successfully displaced team nursing with auxiliaries when nursing elite's new strategy for professionalization converged with managerial interests. The change was implemented because managers believed that RNs were capable of performing a wider range of tasks without the supervisory costs of team nursing. In short, primary nursing and total patient care were believed to be compatible with increasing productivity.

Rank and file RNs cooperated with hospital and nursing elites in reorganizing the work process because reunifying tasks overcame the difficulties they had experienced with auxiliaries at the bedside. Nevertheless, as I have shown through an extended case study at Pacific Hospital, reunifying nursing tasks did not professionalize RNs. On the contrary, the intensification of work that resulted forced RNs to informally engage in strategies to shrink an overextended work jurisdiction, omitting some tasks formerly performed by auxiliaries and shifting others onto the patient and their family. Furthermore, flattening the paranursing hierarchy on hospital wards increased RNs' accountability to administrators and physicians. Continued subordination and the intensification of work ultimately undermined RNs' consent. However, just as the reorganization of the work process had contradictory effects on RNs' work (both overcoming the problems of team nursing and intensifying work), it also had contradictory effects on workplace solidarity, displacing auxiliaries and straining relations with support workers while empowering RNs by eliminating their vulnerability to auxiliaries' substitution.

The historical variation in the organization of nursing work suggests that professionalization and proletarianization are complex social processes that are not necessarily mutually exclusive [1]. As I have shown, neither theory alone captures the complexity of nurses' work. The study has shown that it is possible for professionalizing occupations to pursue and acquire some of the characteristics of full-fledged professions (upgraded skills, responsibility, credentialing) at the same time that the actual organization of work varies considerably. The division of labor in the work process may even be reversed from the pattern that usually occurs with professionalization, that is, task differentiation and the delegation of routine work to nonprofessional workers. If professionalizing occupations are vulnerable to substitution and are unable to adequately control auxiliary workers, they may pursue the divergent strategy of recombining tasks and displacing such workers. Although this strategy allows the dominant occupation to regain control over tasks that were formerly delegated, it does not professionalize work. In an industry and occupational field in which skills are being upgraded, job enlargement and the reassumption of routine tasks intensifies labor and creates an overextended work jurisdiction, an outcome consistent with managerial interests in increasing productivity and with forms of proletarianization that do not require deskilling. Tasks may be recombined and responsibility enlarged at the same time that workers remain vulnerable to exploitation and domination by managers and in the case of nursing, by an elite profession as well.

The complexity in the organization of nurses' work suggests the importance of carefully examining variation in work patterns among occupations claiming professional status. This may require a greater dialogue between the sociology of occupations and professions and the sociology of work and industry. While the former has emphasized empirical and comparative studies of occupations, the latter has focused on the organization of work, typically in nonprofessional work settings where managerial interests more easily prevail over occupational interests. In addition, while elite professions have been over-studied by one specialization, the labor processes of factory workers have preoccupied the other. Yet employment has contracted in manufacturing industries, while the health care industry has expanded to employ a vast and growing work force of subordinate professional and nonprofessional service occupations whose work merits closer examination. As the following epilogue indicates, the organization of nurses' work continues to change as managerial and occupational interests confront new constraints. Primary nursing and the trend toward all-RN staffing have created their own contradictions, undermining the stability of current work patterns.

HOSPITALS AND NURSING IN THE 1990s: THE INSTABILITY OF PRIMARY NURSING AND ALL-RN STAFFING

By the late 1980s, the trend toward all-RN staffing was curtailed by a recurrent RN shortage. Rather than draw attention to the displacement of auxiliaries that underlay staffing problems and the intensification of work on the wards, nursing leaders and the news media focused on the shortage of RNs [2]. While organized nursing may attempt to further its professionalization project by continuing to expand the supply and employment of RNs over nonprofessional nursing workers, this strategy appears to have reached its limits. Not only has the RN shortage broken the momentum, any further expansion of RN staffing over nonprofessional labor faces tough scrutiny by hospital managers ever more pressed to control spiralling health care costs.

Although managers reorganized nursing labor because they believed staffing with a majority of RNs would increase nursing productivity, administrators may now have incentives to retain or reintroduce auxiliaries. Primary nursing and the trend toward an all-RN work force makes RNs indispensable, empowering RNs and undermining management's capacity to substitute auxiliaries. The shortage of RNs and the intensification of work has led RNs to seek higher wages and greater participation in setting staffing guidelines [3]. Consequently, the managerial advantages of staffing with a high proportion of RNs may be undermined by upward pressures on their wages or by RNs' success in lowering the intensity of work by reducing the patient load. With the intractability of the cost crisis, hospitals will pursue staffing patterns that maintain productivity gains and contain labor costs.

In any case, beginning in the late 1980s auxiliaries were more likely to be retained or reintroduced to hospital wards, although in far fewer numbers than existed with team nursing in the 1950s and 1960s [4]. A struggle is now taking place between managers and nursing leaders over the level of auxiliary staffing and control over these workers. Physicians also entered the fray to advocate the introduction of a new type of auxiliary. Although nursing leaders and the ANA defeated the American Medical Association's attempt to introduce "registered care technologists," managers are quietly experimenting with a variety of new possibilities for restructuring the organization of work on hospital wards [5]. In part, they are succeeding because, as we have seen, the interests of nursing leaders do not necessarily coincide with the interests of staff nurses. With intensified work and an overextended work jurisdiction, the employment of some auxiliaries to assist staff RNs with a crushing work load may be welcomed on the wards as long as auxiliaries do not displace RNs or interfere with their control of the work and exercise of responsibility for patient care. As a result, rather than mount across-the-board resistance to the use of auxiliaries, nursing leaders are being forced to revise their definition of professional nursing and to modify formal models of work organization in an effort to accommodate and control the use of auxiliaries.

While the level of RN and auxiliary staffing has clearly been reversed from that prevailing during the team nursing period, it is also apparent that primary nursing and the trend toward all-RN staffing never came close to completely displacing team nursing. A recent study by the American Hospital Association points out that over 35 percent of hospitals continued to identify team nursing as their principal patient care delivery system throughout the 1980s [6]. Nevertheless, this report understates the transition that has taken place. When variants of primary nursing are considered within the same generic category, RN-predominant work patterns with RNs producing the majority of bedside care comprise the most frequently used nursing care delivery system on hospital wards [7]. In addition, what individual hospitals now identify as "team nursing" is unlikely to correspond to the staffing pattern characteristic of the 1950s and 1960s, in which auxiliaries dominated at the bedside. As the American Hospital Association has also reported, 63 percent of all hospital nursing personnel are now RNs, a dramatic reversal from the team nursing period [8]. Still, as hospitals experiment, formal models of team and primary nursing are not only being redefined, they are becoming ambiguous, as the features of each are blended to accommodate a work force composed of RNs and nonprofessional workers. Auxiliaries are now frequently called "nurse extenders" or "patient care assistants" to overcome an association with prior forms of team nursing. While managers are principally interested in meeting their staffing needs with economic efficiency, nursing leaders are concerned that auxiliaries do not replace RNs and that they are restricted to a work jurisdiction under professional nurses' control. Nevertheless, some of the aggravations of team nursing are resurfacing around problems of differentiated work, task delegation, knowledge assimilation, and substitution [9]. Formal nursing models are again unlikely to describe realities on hospital wards, hence sociological studies by outsiders to nursing will be needed to comprehend changes in the organization of work and the continuing dilemmas that are likely to result with further pressures to contain health care costs.

Ironically, the trend toward primary nursing with all-RN staffing is also predisposed to fail due to the fact that nursing's professionalization project will ultimately create a new subdivision of nursing labor at a higher level of credentialing. Although efforts to upgrade RNs' credentialing requirements to the baccalaureate degree have been put on hold because of the recent RN shortage as well as internal conflicts within the occupation, the ANA plans to upgrade nursing by requiring that RNs' licensing be restricted to nurses with four-year degrees. Two-year associate degree RNs, the work force that made the transition to RN-predominant patterns of work possible, are to be downgraded to "associate nurses" who will perform technical tasks under the supervision of "professionally credentialed" RNs responsible for conceptualizing overall nursing care [10]. Although rank and file resistance is to be overcome by exempting associate degree RNs currently practicing, the proposal has split nursing leaders and educators. Community college educators have pointed out that the proposed changes in credentialing and licensure "did not evolve from research identifying differences in competence between graduates of the three types of registered nurse education programs" and are concerned that their graduates will be downgraded to a status formerly occupied by LPNs [11]. Other elite groups are concerned that "nonprofessional" associate nurses will be allowed full membership in the ANA, a strategy recommended by the leadership presumably to prevent hospital unions from organizing associate nurses.

In conclusion, the future organization of nursing is likely to be as controversial and difficult as its past. In examining future changes we can learn more about the processes of professionalization and proletarianization and the realities of professional work under the pressures of cost containment. Medicine may epitomize the professions, but when we consider that RNs and other semiprofessional occupations constitute the majority of professional workers, the challenges these occupations face may be more typical. Their work warrants our further attention.

NOTES

1. For a related argument regarding Canadian nursing, see David Coburn, "The Development of Canadian Nursing: Professionalization and Proletarianization," *International Journal of Health Services* 18(3) (1988): 437-456.
2. "Nurses for the Future: An AJN Supplement," *American Journal of Nursing* (Dec. 1987): 1593-1648; *New York Times*, 7 July 1987, p. 1; CBS television, Dan Rather, "48 Hours," 1 Jan. 1989.
3. *New York Times*, 31 July 1988, p. 1; "As the Storage Takes its Toll on Patient Care, Some Nurses are Speaking up for Better Staffing," *American Journal of Nursing* (Dec. 1987): 1694-1695.
4. Marie Manthey, "Can Primary Nursing Survive?," *American Journal of Nursing* (May 1988): 644-647; Mary A. Blegen, Diane L. Gardner, and Joanne Comi McCloskey, "Survey Results: Who Helps You with Your Work?," *American Journal of Nursing* (Jan. 1992): 26-31.
5. Manthey, "Can Primary Nursing Survive?"; also *New York Times*, 30 June 1988, p. B8; Patricia Brider, "The Move to Patient-Focused Care," *American Journal of Nursing* (Sept. 1992): 27-33.
6. See American Hospital Association, *Hospital Nursing in the '90s* (Chicago: American Hospital Association, 1991), table 18.
7. Individual hospitals may identify their staffing modalities as "primary nursing," "total patient care," or "modular nursing." There are also other terms, but, as Joiner and van Servellen have indicated, all may be considered modifications of primary nursing. See Carl Joiner and Gwen Marram van Servellen, *Job Enrichment in Nursing* (Rockville, Md.: Aspen, 1984), chap. 3.
8. American Hospital Association, *Hospital Nursing in the '90s*, figure 18.
9. "Coast RNs Resist Techs' Takeover of Nursing Tasks," *American Journal of Nursing* (Feb. 1992): 79-86.
10. American Nurses' Association, *American Nurse*, Feb. 1986, p. 5; June 1987, pp. 13-14.
11. American Nurses' Association, *American Nurse*, July-Aug. 1985, pp. 4-5.

Author Index

177

Subject Index